The Science of God-Realization

The Science of God-Realization

Knowing Our True Nature and Our
Relationship With the Infinite

And Other Selected Essays

Roy Eugene Davis

CSA Press • Lakemont, Georgia U.S.A.

CSA Press, Post Office Box 7, Lakemont, Georgia 30552-0001
Telephone 706-782-4723   Fax 706-782-4560
e-mail: csainc@csa-davis.org
Web Site: www.csa-davis.org

The publishing department of Center for Spiritual Awareness.
Offices and retreat center at 151 CSA Lane, Lakemont, Georgia.

PRINTED IN THE UNITED STATES OF AMERICA

*May we be firmly established in flawless knowledge
of our relationship with the Infinite.
May we be steadfast on our awakening path as it
is revealed to us.*

Contents

FOREWORD

The information presented here is neither my own nor new. It is the way of diligent inquiry, constructive living, and attentive spiritual practice that illumines the mind, clarifies awareness, and unveils innate knowledge, qualities, and abilities. Taught by enlightened seers through the ages, it is timeless because it is in accord with universal, impersonal laws or principles of cause and effect. Our innate knowledge and qualities emerge more easily and rapidly when rational thinking and orderly, wholesome living support appropriate spiritual practices.

I am occasionally asked if there are more truth seekers in the world today than in previous eras. Many more people are now interested in spirituality because the human population is increasing and global awakening is accelerated.

What is needed is broad dissemination of accurate information about higher realities; the fact that everyone is a spiritual being and can learn to live effectively in accord with natural laws; and how progressive spiritual growth that will result in liberation of consciousness can be experienced.

Some chapters in this book were first published as magazine articles and have been slightly revised. Several key words in the text are defined in the glossary.

Roy Eugene Davis

Lakemont, Georgia, U.S.A.
November 2001

Publisher's Note: While reading this book, if a word or theme is not comprehended, refer to the glossary. If necessary, also refer to a dictionary for accurate word definitions.

ONE

The Science of God-Realization

science Orderly, disciplined observation, identification, description, and experimental investigation of mundane phenomena or higher realities.

realization Accurate comprehension by direct perception and personal experience.

Acknowledging, understanding, and actually experiencing the reality of God enables the fulfillment of our primary purpose in life to be consummated. If we think that other purposes are more important or demanding, we are mistaken.

Two questions may arise in the mind: 1) If God-realization is really our primary purpose in life, why don't more people aspire to fulfill it?; 2) Among those who do aspire to be God-realized, why are only a few able to accomplish it?

Most people do not aspire to God-realization because they are preoccupied with self-centered interests. When they do think about God, they are inclined to think of having a relationship with God as they imagine God to be, rather than desire to know and experience the reality of God. Among those who aspire to be God-realized, few are able to rise above conditioned states of awareness.

A common difficulty for everyone who has not yet learned to think rationally or whose awareness is ordinary (identified with mental, emotional, and physical states and with external conditions) is their inability to intellectually comprehend the facts about God and the processes of life even when they have access to this information. Why this is so, and how this and all other obstacles to spiritual growth can effectively be removed, will be explained later in this article.

For one who is sincerely intent on God-realization, a most important characteristic to nurture is sustained aspiration to awaken from ordinary states of awareness. When aspiration prevails, one will be inclined to acquire necessary information about how to proceed and to enter into a regimen of further study and practical application that will definitely result in the fulfillment of the heart's desire. (The "heart" is the essence of being which innately yearns to have its awareness restored to wholeness.)

The Reality of God

The one Being, Life, and Power we refer to as God had no origin and will never cease to exist. Its absolute aspect is pure consciousness-existence without attributes. Its expressive aspect, with three attributes which coordinate its manifesting influences, is sometimes referred to as the Oversoul.

The characteristics of the constituent attributes which confine and regulate cosmic forces 1) contribute to luminosity and harmony; 2) are influential when transformative actions occur; 3) manifest as inertia. We can observe the effects of these influences in our environment and in our mind and body.

When these attributes are in a state of equilibrium in the Oversoul, this aspect of God is self-contained. When otherwise, the power of Consciousness streams forth as a vibration: the Word (Greek *Logos*; Sanskrit *Aum* or *Om*), the cause and substance of all that is manifested as the realm of nature. (Meditators are advised to contemplate the meaning and source of the vibration of the power of Consciousness and listen to and merge their attention and awareness in it.)

The vibration of the power of Consciousness influenced by inertia produces a primordial, unified field of space, time, and cosmic forces. From this, the material universe is projected, the processes of which are regulated by the three attributes of the expressive aspect of Consciousness.

Subtle and gross matter emerges from Consciousness. The first stage is a field composed of electrical and magnetic forces, the causal realm through which life forces produce the astral realm. From causal and astral realms, the atomic structure of the material universe is produced.

Light is produced when electrons orbiting the nucleus of atoms are impacted by energy when they receive radiation or collide with other atoms. Intense heat, for instance, will cause the atoms of a substance to collide and their electrons to produce light. When transmitted energy boosts electrons to a higher orbit, their tendency to seek their lowest energy state causes them to drop down to their former level. When this occurs, electrons release excess energy as photons of light. An electron returning to its former level will always release light of a specific wavelength and color. The energy of photons can be detected by instruments that emit a clicking sound when impacted by them.

Only wavelengths that emit red, orange, yellow, green, blue, indigo, and violet colors (which comprise white light) are ordinarily visible to human sight. Red is produced by a low frequency long wave; violet is produced by a high frequency short wave. Wavelengths are electromagnetic frequencies. X-rays and gamma rays are above our range of sight; infrared, microwaves, TV, and radio waves are below it. When we look at things, the colors we see are those which are reflected because they are not absorbed by the object.

Although the universe exists, it is not what most people perceive or think it to be. It is produced by interacting cosmic forces emanated from the primordial field of nature. If we believe otherwise, it is because of our lack of knowledge or our illusions (misperceptions of the facts).

Our Relationship With God

In metaphysical (beyond the physical) teachings, a unit of pure Consciousness is defined as the *true Self* of humans and creatures. Units are individualized as the result of interactions between the Godhead and the field of primordial nature, both of which are aspects of one field of Consciousness. When units of pure consciousness are identified with primordial nature to the extent that awareness is blurred and they "forget" their true nature, they are referred to as souls.

At the innermost level of being the Self is always flawless and serene. It knows what it is and its relationship to God and nature. It is only the blurred aspect of awareness that has to be restored to wholeness.

These facts can be known by diligent inquiry and attentive superconscious meditation practice. All knowledge of the one field of Consciousness and its processes is within us. It can be spontaneously revealed when the mind is calm and awareness is clear.

As a unit of pure consciousness becomes further involved with matter, it takes on sheaths or "bodies" and uses faculties of perception and action composed of material substance to relate to the phenomenal world.

The four characteristics of an individualized unit of pure consciousness are:

- Ego, an illusional sense of selfhood which causes the soul to feel that it is independent—separate from the one field of Consciousness.
- The ability to feel or to be aware of sensation.
- Mind, which records perceptions and processes information. The particularized mind is a unit of Cosmic Mind which is responsive to mental states, thoughts, and desires.
- Intelligence, the power of discernment. When intelligence is purified and highly developed, one is able to easily know the difference between what is true and what is false.

The five faculties of perception are sight, hearing, taste, smell, and touch sensation. The five faculties of action are speech, locomotion or movement in space, manual dexterity, elimination, and reproduction.

While these faculties enable us to relate to a subtle realm or physical world, to be able to have insight into nonphysical realities, intuition, the innate power of direct perception, must be cultivated and used.

Souls incarnated in the physical realm function through five coverings or "bodies":

- The bliss covering, so-called because it enables the Self to experience the sheer joy of being while embodied and the ecstasy of God-communion before complete awakening and realization of the totality of Consciousness.
- The covering of fine material substance through which the embodied Self uses intellectual powers.
- The mental covering, the seat of the mind.
- The astral body, formed of the first three coverings and life forces emanated by the true Self.
- The physical body, composed of material substances.

When attention and awareness of an individualized unit of pure consciousness becomes strongly identified with mental states and objective phenomena, impressions of urges, desires, experiences, and emotional reactions are accumulated in the mind as memories which condition the mind. If such memories influence thinking, feeling, and behavior, more memories with power to influence can be accumulated. Thus a karmic condition results which may cause unwanted effects in the near or distant future.

Although subconscious impressions are recorded in the mind and do not mar the true Self, when the Self falsely thinks and feels itself to be a mind-body being, subconscious influences can be influential. By cultivating superconscious states and viewing memories without emotional reaction, problem-causing mental impressions can be transcended and their potency weakened and neutralized. Then, memories do not adversely influence thoughts, feelings, or behaviors.

The Scientific Way to Facilitate
Self- and God-Realization

Think of yourself as a spiritual scientist intent on learning about, comprehending, and experiencing your true nature and the reality of God. You have the power to do this because you are innately endowed with knowledge of Consciousness and its processes and the capacity to unfold and use exceptional powers of perception. If you have any doubts about your capacity to learn or about having the ability to accomplish this most meaningful purpose, renounce them.

Let us examine some key words which are commonly used to define *science*:

- *Orderly, disciplined observation* is methodical and systematic without disruption or interference. Disciplined thinking, behavior, and intellectual and intuitive analysis can result in accurate perception. This is how an alert truth seeker is advised to study the nature of Consciousness and its processes.
- That which is observed should be *identified*—seen and known as it really is.
- That which is identified should be accurately *described*. If what has been observed cannot be described, it has not been flawlessly perceived.
- *Experimental investigation* makes possible the verification or proving of what has been observed. One who aspires to God-realization must enter into processes that will result in psychological transformation, the removal of physical and mental restrictions to spiritual growth, and clarification and illumination of consciousness.

For many centuries and in many cultures the following self-transformation processes have been discovered, tested by personal experience, and proven to be effective:

- *The way of right living.* Rational, constructive thinking; ethical behaviors; an uncomplicated, wholesome lifestyle; meaningful work skillfully performed; and all other actions which nurture emotional maturity and the actualization of our divine qualities provide a firm foundation for our lives and enables us to have the full support of nature and of God's grace.

Orderly, progressive spiritual growth will naturally occur.

- *The way of knowledge.* Acquiring accurate understanding of the facts of life and living in accord with essentials. Lower knowledge, of the mundane realm, is necessary to have in order to function effectively. Higher knowledge, of the one field of Consciousness and its processes, is liberating because it enables us to be Self- and God-realized. To more easily acquire higher knowledge which will eventually blossom as wisdom, use your powers of discriminative intelligence to clearly discern the difference between your true Self and ordinary or conditioned states of awareness. Be aware of the fact that, as a spiritual being, you are superior to your physical, emotional, and mental states.

- *The way of devotion.* Ardent attachment or loyalty rather than sentimental emotionalism. To what are you devoted? Be devoted to right living and to knowing the truth about your relationship with God. When you pray or meditate, be completely devoted to the process and to the ideal of experiencing the culmination of the process.

- *The way of attentive contemplative meditation.* Practiced by withdrawing attention from the senses, emotions, and mental states in order to elicit transcendent, superconscious states. It is the direct way to Self- and God-realization. To be effective, diligent practice of contemplative meditation should be supported by right living, the acquisition of lower and higher knowledge, and unswerving devotion to cherished ideals.

The Liberating Results of Right Endeavor

When knowledge-based, right endeavor is diligent, the mind becomes orderly, intellectual powers improve, emotions are calm and balanced, physical health is easily maintained, and supportive resources, relationships, events, and circumstances spontaneously emerge. Living is then enjoyable and successful. At deeper levels, subtle changes occur that result in the unveiling and unfoldment of innate spiritual qualities.

- Vital forces, once dormant, awaken and move upward in the body, refine the nervous system and brain, strengthen the immune system, weaken the soul's attachment to the body, and enable the truth seeker to become aware of the astral body and its characteristics and processes.
- The mind is purified and illumined by the radiance of the true Self. Delusions and illusions are banished. Destructive subconscious conditionings are weakened and dissolved; the soul force formerly confined by them is released.
- Intellectual powers are enhanced, enabling the devotee to comprehend the reality of Consciousness, its categories of self-manifestation, and its processes.
- Intuition is unveiled. The soul's ability to know whatever it wants to know, unsupported by the senses, allows direct perception of the true Self and the reality of God.

It can be helpful for a sincere truth seeker to be assisted by a spiritually enlightened teacher who has awakened through the stages of spiritual growth and can provide knowledge and encouragement. In the absence of this ideal relationship, one should acquire accurate knowledge from available, reliable sources and skillfully apply it.

This scientific approach to God-realization is for everyone because the procedures are universally applicable. It does not matter that psychological characteristics of people in diverse cultures may be different because of their personal histories and acquired beliefs. At the innermost level of their being, the spiritual essence is the same. In Western cultures, the word *psyche* (Latin, from Greek *psūkhe*, soul or spiritual essence) is usually defined from a materialistic point of view as "a mind functioning as the center of thought, feeling, and behavior consciously or unconsciously adjusting and relating the body to its social and physical environment." Knowing that we are units of one field of Consciousness using a mind and a physical body, we need not be limited by mental or physical states, acquired beliefs, or the opinions of others.

What is of primary importance is personal resolve to elicit innate divine qualities by skillfully doing what is necessary to consciously know our relationship with the Infinite and to be fully realized.

Affirmation
I am firmly resolved to unfold my innate divine
qualities as I skillfully do what is necessary to allow
my potential to consciously know my relationship with
the Infinite to be fully realized.

There is a fundamental purpose for our lives. To recognize it we must understand where life comes from and where it is going. We must look beyond our immediate goals to what we ultimately want to accomplish and think about life's highest potential for development.

– Paramahansa Yogananda

TWO

The Simplicity of Self-Discovery

When our awareness is strongly identified with conditioned mental states, suffering and unhappiness—mild, medium, or intense—may be experienced. The only permanent solution to this problem is to nurture spiritual growth until illumination of consciousness is realized.

The primary cause of human suffering and unhappiness is an illusional sense of separation between the real Self and God. It is only the habit of identifying with mental, emotional, and physical states and objective phenomena that causes and sustains the illusion of separate existence. When this error is corrected, enlightenment is spontaneously experienced.

To be enlightened is to know that we are spiritual beings and have accurate, comprehensive knowledge of the infinite field of Consciousness and the processes of life.

When we mistakenly presume our pure-conscious Self to be a mortal, mind-body entity, our awareness is ordinary. It is contracted, limited, fragmented, and influenced by subconscious conditionings, subliminal drives and inclinations, unsettled emotions, and emotional reactions to our thoughts, moods, and external events. It is only at the surface of our awareness that confusion can exist; at the core of our being we are serene, knowledgeable, and whole.

Even though painful conditions can often be somewhat relieved by various practical means, to merely reduce discomfort without discovering and removing its cause allows possibilities of near or future unpleasantness to exist.

Suffering is not "God's will" for us, nor is it necessary for emotional or spiritual growth. Effects have causes which correspond to them. We can do practical things to remove the underlying causes of distress while also engaging in practices which will quicken our spiritual growth.

The first positive choice to make is to be optimistic in spite of existing conditions. Cheerfulness and optimism enable us to be receptive to new possibilities, energize mind and body, and strengthen the immune system. Pessimistic mental attitudes, sadness, and feelings of despair constrict awareness and weaken the mind and body. We do not need a "reason" to be optimistic. If we are habitually pessimistic, it is only because we choose to dramatize this mental state. If we are inclined to blame circumstances or the behaviors of others for our mental and emotional states, we need to grow to emotional maturity by choosing to be responsible for our thoughts, feelings, and circumstances.

To free your mind, liberate your vital forces, and enhance your life, do these things:

- Discover and remove causes of physical distress while nurturing health and well-being. A healthy, long, physical life wisely lived with conscious intention will provide many opportunities to fulfill your meaningful purposes and accomplish the ultimate degree of spiritual growth.
- Heal emotional unrest by nurturing total health and well-being and cultivating peace of mind and soul contentment. Refuse to be emotionally disturbed by transitory events, the behaviors of others, or unpleasant memories. Avoid worry.
- Eradicate mental confusion by cultivating habits of rational thinking and decisiveness. Meditate on a regular schedule to reduce stress, calm the mind, and clarify your awareness.
- Master attention by will power, improving your powers of concentration, and focusing thoughts and actions on matters related to meaningful purposes. Mastery of attention, will power, concentration, and creativity are related to the front lobes of the brain. Practice keeping your awareness centered in this part of the brain when meditating and when engaged in routine activities. Concentrate mostly on essential matters; disregard nonessential matters. Obtain sufficient rest. Choose

a balanced, nutritious (preferably vegetarian) diet plan.

- Be assured of supportive relationships by supporting others while maintaining your integrity. Be self-reliant and confident rather than dependent and insecure.

- Eliminate poverty and restrictions by being mindful that necessary resources, fortunate events, and ideal circumstances will harmoniously manifest in accord with your ability to be receptive to them. Be thankful for the good fortune you now have. Help yourself to the extent that you can while relying on the Source from which everything emerges.

- Banish addictive tendencies and pain-causing subconscious conditionings by resisting their influences and weaken and neutralize them with constructive thoughts, feelings, and actions. Don't think or say that you are a victim of influences or circumstances over which you have no control. Don't think or say that "your karma" (subconscious conditionings and acquired mental attitudes) is "bad" or too strong to overcome, or that your life is determined by "unfriendly" planetary aspects. You are not weak or helpless; the full power of God is within you at the deepest level of your being. Acquire the knowledge you need to function effectively and use it. Choose to be superconscious rather than allow your awareness to be dominated by subconscious states and debilitating habits. When your will to live and to prevail is stronger than your inclination to be passive or semiconscious, it will be easier to overcome and rise above conditions which were formerly restrictive.

- Acquire insight into your true nature and your relationship with the Infinite and a comprehensive understanding of both metaphysical and mundane laws of cause and effect. Outgrow small-mindedness. Your clear perceptions of the processes of life will enable you to live freely, creatively, and joyfully without strong attachments or aversions.

You are not in this world to nurture ordinary states of awareness or emotionally dependent personal relationships, occasionally think about your relationship with the Infinite, or hope that spiritual growth may eventually occur without having to do anything to nurture it. You are here to awaken to complete Self- and God-realization while skillfully relating to the human condition and rendering useful service to others and the planet.

God is our origin and true essence. While we play our roles for a few years in space and time, we abide in eternity—a transcendent field of reality which had no beginning and will have no end. We are one with a field of Consciousness that has no discernible boundaries and our minds are units of a Cosmic Mind which responds to our thoughts and emotional states and the impulses of our desires. To become aware of what we are in relationship to the wholeness of life and how our thoughts, emotions, and desires influence our experiences enables us to live effectively and understand the subtle causes that produce our circumstances.

Because we are individualized units of the infinite field of Consciousness and our minds are units of one Mind, we are one with everyone and with all aspects of life. Because we are one with the cosmos, when we think, feel, and live in accord with the laws which govern nature's processes, we discover, by insight and personal experience, that ideal place in life where we can most efficiently function and have the full support of the forces and attributes of nature.

Self-discovery immediately eliminates mental confusion and emotional conflict and makes effective living possible. What is the Self that is to be discovered, and how can it be known and realized?

Our true Self is the essence of our being, not the illusional sense of selfhood with which many people are identified and mistakenly presume themselves to be. For a person whose awareness is almost always identified with the physical body and the senses, personality characteristics, random thoughts and feelings, and circumstances and relationships, their real Selfhood may be difficult to comprehend—and to experience.

It is not uncommon to hear someone refer to "their soul," as though their spiritual essence was something other than themselves. This erroneous concept of selfhood is the major obstacle to Self-discovery. If authentic spiritual awakening is to be experienced, the first constructive thing to do is to acquire an intellectual understanding of what the Self is in relationship to the larger field of Consciousness and to the mind, body, and environment. Without this understanding, even sincere truth seekers are inclined to wander aimlessly through life and are almost certain to fail to accomplish anything of real value. Their well-intentioned spiritual practices may be unsuitable for their needs. If they have knowledge of useful spiritual practices, because of their egocentric (illusional self-centered condition) they may not be able to derive much benefit from their application.

Because of blurred awareness, emotional unrest, or perhaps because of curiosity about mundane phenomena, you were born into this world in a physical body. You did not incarnate because you committed a grievous (serious) wrong act that needs to be punished; you are here because you forgot your true nature and relationship to the Infinite or desired to participate in the processes of life. When you are Self-realized, you can knowledgeably and enjoyably participate until you depart from this world in accord with the trends of your spiritual destiny.

To Discover Your True Self, Cultivate Nonjudgmental
Awareness and Intellectual and Intuitive Discernment

By contemplation on pure consciousness, innate knowledge is definitely revealed. By contemplation on the heart [the reality of being], knowledge of it is revealed. By contemplation on the self-existent reality of Consciousness, one acquires the ability to discern the difference between it and relative experiences. – *Pantanjali's yoga-sutras 3:34–36*

That which is discovered is directly perceived. Although you have always been a spiritual being, until you actually know it, it may seem that you are other than what you really are. Even when you are not fully aware of the essence of your being, you can be aware that you are other than the thoughts you think, the moods you experience, the various sensations you have, and the physical body which is constantly changing while you observe the transformations which occur.

Detach your attention from thoughts and emotions and calmly observe your states of awareness, thoughts, imaginings, memories, moods, desires, urges, and physical sensations. Discern the difference between you as the observer and ordinary, conditioned states of awareness. If you are not immediately able to fully identify with your true nature you will at least know the difference between it and what you observe. Many people are so completely identified with physical and emotional states, personality characteristics, and habitual modes of thinking that they believe themselves to be mere mortal, mind-body beings. The events and circumstances of their lives then tend to be determined by causes which are not understood and over which (they may believe) they have little or no control.

Mastery of attention is the key to Self-discovery. When sitting quietly and contemplating your real nature and your relationship to the one field of Consciousness, or when meditating, endeavor to discern the truth of your real nature and infinite Consciousness. Remain alert. Notice the subtle or obvious shifts of viewpoint and adjustments of states of awareness that occur.

When experiencing constructive changes in states of awareness there may be occasions of confusion or emotional unrest because former states of awareness, feelings, and concepts with which you were familiar are being replaced by new states. Your sense of Self and your understanding of yourself and all that you see around you is changing because you are awakening from conditioned states of awareness. Your mind is being illumined and your awareness is being clarified. Some of the activities you formerly enjoyed and personal habits and relationships you thought were meaningful may no longer be of interest to you. You may have to learn to appropriately adapt to circumstances and to family members, friends, and others while maintaining your inner awareness and privately attending to spiritual practices to allow your innate capacities to unfold.

Observe your state of awareness immediately after awakening from sleep, before thoughts and feelings become influential. Notice that you are peaceful, desireless, and problem-free. At the core of your being you are always like this. Train yourself to maintain this state at all times. You will then be serene, make wise choices, and accomplish purposes more easily. By attentive practice, regardless of what you are doing or what is occurring around you, you will always be Self- and God-aware.

Meditate With Conscious Intention

Undoubtedly the mind is unsteady and difficult to restrain, but it can be mastered by yoga practice and nonattachment ... by the devotee whose self-conscious nature is subjected to the soul's will, by right endeavor and proper means, it is possible to accomplish.

– Bhagavad Gita 6:35,36

Daily meditation to elicit deep relaxation, calm the mind, and clear awareness will result in gradual, progressive spiritual growth. To make your practice more beneficial, after resting for a while in the clearly aware, calm state, engage in Self-enquiry by contemplating (directing your attention to) your core essence of being. Disregard thoughts and feelings: gently endeavor to discern your true Self as a pure-conscious being unsupported by concepts or emotional states. Remember that you do not have to try to "become" what you already are. You have only to acknowledge and identify your awareness with what you are.

If concentration is difficult, if thoughts or moods interrupt your meditative endeavors, practice a technique to involve your attention and calm the breath and the flows of life force in your body. When breathing is smooth and refined and your life forces are harmonized, mental processes are pacified, emotions are settled, and concentration is easier to maintain.

You may use a meditation technique that appeals to you: observe your natural breathing rhythm, listen to a pleasant word or word-phrase (mantra); listen to subtle sound in the inner ear; gaze into the space between your eyebrows (the spiritual eye center). If you are a kriya yoga initiate, practice the basic pranayama techniques and supplemental procedures. Use a technique until it is no longer needed, then sit in the deep silence, aware of the essence of your being and the reality of the ocean of Consciousness of which you are an individualized unit.

By practicing meditation like this, your innate urge to have your awareness restored to wholeness will direct the process. At this stage, personal endeavor ceases: the redemptive influence of interior grace prevails. Remain alert and observant rather than sit passively in a semiconscious state.

How to Contemplate for Self-Discovery

When the mind has been calmed by meditation practice (or at any other time when the mind is calm), analyze what you are. At first, thoughts (concepts and opinions) and feelings may be present. You can know that these are not what you really are because you observe them. They arise, then subside, driven by restless wave-like movements at unconscious levels. When thoughts and feelings are dormant (or ignored), all that remains is awareness of "I am" or "I exist." What is this "I-ness" of you that self-exists? Explore it at its core until you realize it.

There may be fleeting moments of insight which quickly become obscured by thoughts or moods. Your attention may wander. Heaviness or mental dullness may interfere with attempts to concentrate. Thoughts about the usefulness or the "rightness" of the process may surface in the mind: Is it going to work? Do I have the right to do this? If it can be done, why haven't more people done it? If I do discover the truth of what I am, will my life be changed, and if it will, what will the changes be like? Will my lifestyle, behaviors, and relationships be different? When you are engaged in meditative contemplation, thoughts are obstacles to Self-discovery. Even the intellect, by which concepts are understood, will be transcended when your purified intuitive powers enable you to directly perceive and know your true Self.

Adhere to a Regimen of Orderly,
Wholesome, Purposeful Living

There is a fundamental purpose for our lives. To recognize it, we must understand where life comes from and where it is going. We must look beyond our immediate goals to what we ultimately want to accomplish.
– Paramahansa Yogananda

Your Self-discovery endeavors are likely to be more successful when your life is well-ordered, wholesome, and purposeful. While it is true that living like this is easier when one is already spiritually awake, choosing to live like this before one is fully conscious nurtures and supports the awakening process.

During a private conversation with Paramahansa Yogananda, I expressed my desire to be Self-realized. He said, "Roy, you have to live anyway [whether you are Self-realized or not]; why not live in the highest way?"

You do not have to wait until you are spiritually enlightened to experience the benefits of "right" living. Choose to be self-reliant, soul-determined, and responsible for your thoughts, moods, private behaviors, and actions and their consequences. Knowing that your mind is a unit of Cosmic Mind which is responsive to your mental states and thoughts, be optimistic, think rationally, and learn by experimentation how the mental laws of cause and effect produce predictable results. Knowing that peace of mind; nutritious food; cleanliness; appropriate, regular exercise; and a balanced routine of activity and rest nurtures physical health and well-being, choose behaviors which will enable you to be physically healthy and vital. Knowing that purposeful living makes life more meaningful and enables you to live effectively, be purposeful. Purposefulness, being decisive and intentional about what you do and why you do it, will enable you to be attentive and to wisely use your energies and resources. Cultivate mental states, states of awareness, behaviors, and relationships which will enable you to be prosperous, fulfilled, and happy. At all times, remain Self- and God-aware.

There is no separation between spiritual and material realities. Consciousness is the only, one, undivided reality. Subtle aspects of Consciousness emanate its gross aspects (its vibrations manifest material phenomena). The physical universe is produced and sustained by interactions of cosmic forces which arise within the one field of Consciousness. According to the current speculation of cosmologists, only five percent of the energy (material substance) of the universe is visible. Ninety-five percent, some of which is referred to as "dark matter" which is not influenced by gravity, can be detected by special instruments or is only presumed to exist.

Orderly living improves receptivity to the supportive forces of nature and contributes to psychological and physical health. Absence of physical discord, mental conflict, and emotional unrest allows the body's life forces to flow smoothly and the nervous system to become refined. Spiritual growth can then occur more rapidly.

Recognize and Renounce or Transcend
These Obstacles to Self-Discovery

First seek realization of the wholeness of God, and knowledge of the orderly processes of life, and all of these things [whatever is needed] will be provided for you. – *Gospel of Matthew 6:33 / Modern translation*

The primary obstacle to enlightenment is identification with and attachment to the illusional sense of self-identity. Until this is overcome, the following attachments, which may be weak, mild, or strong, may also be obstacles to spiritual growth:

• *Attachment to physical states, things, circumstances, and relationships.* To overcome them, know your body as the vehicle through which you express. Maintain it in a healthy condition without thinking or feeling that you are the body. Use material things wisely. Avoid emotional dependence on them but do not be averse to relating to the physical universe. Enjoy and nurture supportive relationships while allowing others freedom to grow to their full potential. Knowing that you will eventually depart from this realm, maintain a cosmic perspective in regard to your actions and relationships.

- *Attachment to mental concepts and emotional states.* Renounce ideas and opinions which are invalid and all illusions, especially in regard to your real nature, God, and religious or philosophical theories. Discover what is true and live in accord with that knowledge. Be devoted to God and your spiritual path while avoiding excessive emotionalism that distorts the intellect and blurs intuition. Don't presume that pious thoughts and pleasant feelings are signs of spiritual awareness.

- *Attachment to meditative perceptions.* Even devotees who are spiritually advanced may not awaken to Self-realization because of fascination with and attachment to subjective visual or auditory phenomena, ecstatic states, or refined superconscious perceptions.

Until Self-realization is flawless, various perceptions may be had when meditating. One may become aware of inner light, which may be brilliant and clear, appear as patterns of colors, or in which dreamlike "visions" may occur. The clear light, produced by the brain, indicates mental and emotional calmness. Patterns of color may indicate the influences of life force frequencies. Dreamlike perceptions are caused by thoughts, emotional unrest, and subliminal influences.

Boundaries that enable meditators to ordinarily recognize the difference between things may seem to dissolve, resulting in a sense of the oneness or wholeness of life. An overwhelming feeling of love and compassion may be experienced. Surges of life force may cause mild or strong feelings of ecstasy. Expanded states of awareness may be awesome. One may err in thinking that the ultimate stage of spiritual awakening has been accomplished.

A devotee who is intent on illumination of consciousness should endeavor to discern the difference between that which is observed and the observer, between what is perceived and what one is. All that is observed is impermanent and subject to change; what one is as a spiritual being is permanent and unchangeable.

Guidelines to Enlightened Living

Evidence that enlightenment is flawless is that knowledge of our true Self and the wholeness of life is always present and we are able to live efficiently, effectively, and enjoyably.

Some characteristics of commitment to the enlightenment path are described in the Bhagavad Gita (16:1–3):

Fearlessness, purity of heart [motive], abiding in Self-knowledge, charitableness, self-restraint, offering all actions to God [for the good of others and of nature], study of sacred texts, disciplined living, honesty, harmlessness, truthfulness, absence of anger, renunciation, serenity, freedom from faultfinding, compassion for all beings, absence of cravings, gentleness, modesty, steadiness, vigor, forgiveness, fortitude, purity, absence of malice and pride.

These characteristics are spontaneously expressive when one is Self-realized. If they are not already actualized, they should be cultivated.

Some mental characteristics which are incompatible with spiritual aspiration are hypocrisy, arrogance, pride, anger, violence, insolence, and ignorance.

Hypocrisy can be replaced with sincerity. Arrogance and pride can be replaced with humility. Anger can be replaced with self-control, patience, and understanding. Inclinations to be violent (forcefully harmful) can be replaced with kindness and supportive actions. Insolence (abrasive speech and/or behavior) can be replaced with appropriate speech and actions. Ignorance can be replaced with knowledge.

Wholesome living and regular interludes of meditation practiced to the stage of superconsciousness will elicit soul qualities and greatly contribute to psychological transformation. Self-analysis, adjustments in mental attitude, and behavior modification are also necessary spiritual practices. Every constructive action we perform with conscious intention is spiritual practice that can banish the physical and mental obstacles to Self- and God-realization.

The basic guideline to enlightened living is to think, feel, and act in ways which allow innate soul qualities to emerge while avoiding thoughts, feelings, and actions which suppress them. After having acquired knowledge, let your common sense, intuition, and personal experiences guide you.

The Life-Enhancing Results of Authentic Self-Knowledge

Having an idea about what you are is helpful, as are intuitive insights. Self-realization occurs when a shift of viewpoint allows you to understand that your former ideas about your true nature were illusions. With this adjustment of viewpoint, you are aware that you are, and have ever been, a spiritual being. You are also able to clearly comprehend the reality of God and may be pleasantly surprised to discover that most of your former ideas about God were illusions that occurred because your mind was confused, awareness was blurred, and intuition was suppressed. Innate knowledge of the cosmos and your relationship to it blossoms.

• You no longer struggle to overcome difficult situations; you easily see through them, flawlessly discern their causes, and intuitively know solutions.
• With spiritual awakening, the obstacles and troubles, which once seemed so formidable, cease to exist.
• Peace of mind replaces discontent.
• Physical and emotional health replace illness and conflict.
• Purposefulness and skillfully performed actions replace uncertainty and ineptitude. Life is lived freely and joyously.
• Prosperity replaces poverty.
• Final awakening to full liberation of consciousness occurs easily and spontaneously.

The solution to all of the problems and to misfortune and pain related to the ordinary human condition is to be spiritually awake. If you are not yet awake to the truth of your Self, wake up. If you are partially awake, continue to contemplate what is true until it is fully realized. If you are completely awake, abide there.

Affirmation
Ever alert and attentive, I acknowledge and
identify with the pure essence of my being.

He who knows others is wise;
He who knows himself is enlightened.
– Lao-tsu (604 – 531 B.C.E.)

THREE

In the Sanctuary of Silence
How to Practice Meditation Effectively

Contemplative meditation is a direct way to God-realization. When practiced effectively, attention is removed from sensory and mental involvements, allowing awareness to be restored to its natural, clear state.

Yoga [awareness of being unified with one field of Consciousness] is realized when fluctuations in individualized awareness cease. Then, the seer [the perceiver] abides in the Self [essence of being]. When otherwise, the seer's attention is inclined to identify with the [various] modifications of the mind. – *Patanjali's yoga-sutras 1:2 – 4*

The primary influences that modify mental processes are: 1) valid information that is presently in the mind; 2) erroneous ideas; 3) illusions (misperceived information); 4) sleep states; and 5) memories. When the mind is thus modified, irrational thinking results and awareness is fragmented.

Millions of people meditate for a variety of reasons. Many of them practice it because they appreciate the psychological and physical benefits that result: reduction of stress; mental peace and emotional calmness; rational thinking; improved powers of concentration; strengthening of the body's immune system; relief from anxiety-related disabilities, addictions, and pain; and an enhanced sense of well-being.

When superconscious meditation is regularly practiced and wholesome lifestyle regimens are adhered to, spiritual growth is satisfying and spontaneously progressive.

Contemplative meditation is practiced by concentrating on a chosen object or ideal until distinctions between meditating and the object of meditation are absent.

Concentration may be focused on:

- God, or one's concept of God.
- One's true Self or essence of being.
- Inwardly perceived light.
- A preferred word or word-phrase (mantra) or inner sound that can be naturally heard.
- Any other preferred object or ideal that supports aspiration to be more fully awake.

The purpose of directing attention to an object or ideal is to remove it from mundane circumstances and emotional and mental states so that clear awareness can prevail. The meditator can then proceed to elicit superconscious states.

Superconscious states transcend ordinary states of awareness. Whatever we perceive leaves an impression in the mind which may be harmless, harmful, or constructive. Superconscious influences are always entirely constructive. They weaken harmful subconscious impressions and purify the mind, thus thinking can be more rational and intellectual powers improve.

Superconscious influences which prevail during and after meditation also refine the brain and nervous system, allowing soul awareness to more easily express. When the brain and nervous system are refined and the mind is calm, the radiance of the true Self is unveiled.

How to Meditate Effectively

Meditation practice is easy, enjoyable, and beneficial. For many people, the most difficult part of the process is deciding to do it and adhering to a regular practice schedule.

Choose a time of day that is most suitable for you. Early morning is a good time because it allows you to begin your day relaxed, mentally refreshed, and spiritually aware. Any quiet place where you will not be disturbed can be used.

- Sit upright in a comfortable chair, poised and alert. If you prefer a cross-legged, seated posture, this is all right.

- Close your eyes. Relax. Acknowledge your spiritual essence in relationship to the Infinite. Direct your attention to the space between and above your eyebrows and the front part of your brain.
- If meditation flows spontaneously, let it occur. If it does not spontaneously flow, use a technique to focus concentration. This can be silent prayer or any of the techniques described in this chapter.
- When you are calm and your awareness is somewhat clear, disregard the technique and let the meditation process flow as determined by your innate urge to have your awareness restored to wholeness. Stay alert and attentive.
- Conclude the practice session when you decide to do so.

New meditators are advised to sit for 15 to 20 minutes or a little longer if alert attention can be maintained. After a few days or a few weeks, when proficiency is acquired, it will be easy to sit for 30 minutes to an hour. If longer sessions result in excessive preoccupation with subjective states or disinterest in the performance of duties, one should not meditate longer than 30 minutes until a balance of interest in both subjective and objective matters can be easily maintained.

Helpful Meditation Techniques You Can Use

A helpful meditation technique can enable you to relax the body, calm the mind, and focus your attention so that you can meditative effectively. Disregard the technique when you no longer need it.

- The easiest method is to observe your breathing. Be aware of the air flowing into and out of your nostrils.
- Listening to a mantra is another easy method. If you do not yet use a mantra, choose one that appeals to you. The word "God" can be used. The words "Om–God" or "Om–Peace" can be used as two word mantras. If using one word, mentally recite it when you inhale or exhale. If using two words, men-

tally recite the first word when you breath in and the second word when you breathe out. Keep your awareness identified with the spiritual eye center as you do this. As you progress, instead of mentally reciting the mantra, mentally "listen" to it as though it is emerging in your mind and awareness.

- If you perceive inner light, let it attract your attention.
- If you hear a subtle sound in your ears or in your head, use it as a mantra.
- Some meditators prefer to mentally pray for Self- and God-awareness, then sit quietly in silence. Any method you use that enables you to internalize your attention and remove it from mental and emotional states can be helpful.

The Progressive Stages of Meditation Practice

Attentive meditation practice progresses through these six stages. Memorize them so you will know how to proceed.

- Sitting in an upright posture that is comfortable.
- Eliciting relaxation and balancing flows of life force in the body to calm the mind.
- Internalization of attention.
- Concentration on the chosen object or ideal.
- Concentration which flows smoothly without interruption is real meditation.
- The culmination of practice.

When meditating, endeavor to experience a superconscious state. Avoid preoccupation with moods, memories, thoughts, or problems. Leave all mundane concerns at the door of your meditation chamber. Rather than try to "get something" from your practice, renounce your illusional sense of selfhood if you have it, and you will have worthwhile results.

Also avoid attachment to pleasant feelings and other subjective perceptions. Disregard and rise above them. Focus your attention on the purpose of meditation practice: to elicit and explore superconscious states.

Preliminary states of superconsciousness may be blended with an ordinary self-conscious state. Your awareness may be partially clear and you will be peaceful while thoughts and emotions are not yet calm. Eventually, when restlessness no longer stimulates thoughts and emotions, superconsciousness will be transcendent. Even at this stage, your sense of being an individualized unit of a larger field of consciousness may result in a sense of God-communion rather than God-oneness.

Persist until you are aware of being free in inner space, aware that your sense of individuality is like a bubble in the ocean of God, then continue to persist until only oneness is realized.

When concentrating on a mantra, inner light or sound, or contemplating the possibility of transcending all subjective objects of perception, your awareness may be so absorbed in the process that a duration of complete identification with the object or ideal is experienced. Later, you will remember that, during that interval of time, you were only aware of being that which was formerly observed. This temporary state of "oneness of awareness with an object of concentration" is useful. During that interval, thoughts are absent and your awareness is not fragmented. It is not liberating, however, because it requires an object for its support.

Beyond the superconscious state of "oneness of awareness with an object of concentration" is the transcendent state of "clear awareness of existence-being" which does not require a supporting object of perception.

Beyond the state of "clear awareness of existence-being" is the stage of Self-knowledge which allows you to be aware of your true nature and higher realities when you are engaged in ordinary activities and relationships.

To be able to easily experience "oneness with an object of concentration" is an indication of accomplished meditation practice. To experience "existence-being" without a supporting object is an indication of highly developed powers of discernment. To always be aware of your true nature and higher realities, whether meditating or not, is a superior level of Self-realization.

Most people usually experience various states of modified awareness and are only interested in satisfying self-centered desires and having mundane relationships. Skillful meditators who aspire to Self- and God-realization elicit superconscious states that enable them to transcend the ordinary human condition. They live effectively without being unduly influenced by external circumstances.

After having had a few transcendent realizations, avoid thinking that you must talk about your experiences or must go forth to teach others. Talking about personal experiences will distract your attention and dissipate your spiritual forces. Trying to teach before you are established in Self-knowledge will be of little or no value to those you try to help. Until you are competent to teach others, if they seem to be interested in learning, give them some helpful literature or recommend a teacher or teaching. If they are sincere, they will continue their studies, adopt wholesome lifestyle regimens, and engage in spiritual practices in accord with their ability and capacity.

The subtle processes of meditation can only be known by personal experience. I learned about meditation more than fifty years ago; learned how to meditate a few months later after I met Paramahansa Yogananda; and acquired knowledge of the subtle processes by attentive practice.

It is important that our metaphysical study and meditation be balanced by endeavors to live effectively. The exceptional powers of concentration and perception acquired by skillful meditation can be constructively used in everyday circumstances and the self-discipline that is required to live effectively can be applied to meditation practice.

Meditation and contemplation should not be indulged to escape from responsibilities. The improved understanding that results from attentive meditation and contemplation of higher realities provides an expanded view of life, its processes, and real purposes.

Helpful Meditation Routines

A clearly defined meditation routine will enable you to sit, begin your practice, and proceed with purposeful intention. If you do not have a clearly defined routine, you may be inclined to sit and wait to see what will happen. Your attention may wander as you sit passively, allowing thoughts, memories, and moods to dominate your awareness. When you are a skillful, experienced meditator, you will not need a specific practice routine: you will immediately flow into meditation, intuitively do what is necessary to elicit clear states of consciousness, and be responsive to impulses of grace as they arise from the core of your being. Until then, a helpful routine can keep your attention focused. Occasionally modify it as your understanding and skills improve.

• Schedule a specific time when you will meditate. You will then look forward to meditating at that time. Indecision and procrastination are obstacles to success in any endeavor.
• If you can have a private place in your home set aside for your inner work, this can be helpful. It may be a small room or a place in a room that is used only for this purpose. When you go there, you will be able to immediately ignore all mundane matters and direct your attention inward. You may want to have a small altar, a picture of a saint or your guru, or other items that elicit feelings of devotion.
• When you first sit, close your eyes, and open your mind and heart (being) to the Infinite.
• If you use a meditation technique, practice it now.
• When sitting in the silence, if you notice that your attention is wavering, gently use will power to focus your concentration. Or use a meditation technique until you no longer need it.
• If you use several techniques during an extended session, use them in the sequence that best serves your purpose.
• When ending your practice session, pause a few moments to be aware of your thoughts, physical sensations, and relationship to God and the world. Know and feel (at the core of your

being) that you are in harmony with the processes of life and that they support and provide for you.

Visualize your enlightened awareness blending with the collective consciousness of everyone, everywhere.

Acknowledge all souls everywhere and wish for them their spiritual fulfillment.

On a regular schedule, (once each week, twice each month, or once each month) meditate longer than you usually do. Also meditate longer on special occasions: during special days of a holy season, on your birthday, the start of a new year, or to mark the anniversary of a unique event that was spiritually significant for you. If you usually meditate for 30 minutes, on these occasions meditate for an hour. If you usually meditate for an hour, meditate for two hours or more. These sessions will provide opportunities for you to abide in the sanctuary (sacred abode) of silence.

Affirmation
Daily, I reverently enter the sanctuary of silence
and am there fulfilled.

The practitioner of yoga should contemplate the supreme Reality, in solitude, alone, with mind and body controlled. Established in a firm, comfortable meditation posture, in a clean, quiet place, there intent on practice with thoughts and senses subdued, craving nothing, the devotee should meditate to purify the mind. Holding the body, head, and neck erect, motionless, gazing into the spiritual eye, serene, fearless, self-controlled, concentrating on the supreme Reality [only], one should sit, devoted to the highest realization. – *Bhagavad Gita 6:10 – 14*

FOUR

How to Experience Authentic Spiritual Growth

Spiritual growth is authentic when we are increasingly more peaceful, healthy-minded, effectively functional, and aware of our true nature in relationship to the wholeness of life. It is rapid and soul-satisfying when appropriate endeavors to facilitate it are empowered by unwavering aspiration to be spiritually awake.

To experience authentic spiritual growth, do these things:

- Discipline your thoughts, emotions, and actions. Psychological transformation that may be necessary will occur and you will be able to more easily grow to emotional maturity and live effectively.
- Acquire comprehensive knowledge about God, your true nature, and your relationship with the wholeness of life. Then, as your spiritual growth progresses, you will be able to more easily understand what is occurring. As intellectual knowledge is acquired, your intuitive powers will enable you to recognize the truth of what you are examining.
- Live a natural, wholesome, uncomplicated life. Nurture your physical health by cultivating a "health consciousness" and by adhering to appropriate regimens of self-care: exercise, rest and relaxation, and a low (but sufficient) calorie, nutrition-rich diet plan (vegetarian foods are recommended).
- Allow your ego to be purified.
- Cultivate and use your powers of intellect and intuition to discern the difference between your essence of being and ordinary states of awareness.
- Use meditation techniques to elicit physical relaxation, mental and emotional calmness, and clear states of awareness.

The Seven Stages of Spiritual Growth

Progressive stages of soul awakening can be discerned by observing psychological characteristics and behaviors. We can then know our present stage of spiritual growth. By adopting the characteristics and behaviors which correspond to higher levels, we can awaken from ignorance to knowledge. We do not have to be limited by karma, genetic factors, real or imagined planetary influences, or environmental circumstances.

The seven categories of states of consciousness are related to the chakras or vital centers in the spine and brain through which soul awareness expresses. Until one's enlightenment is complete, the psychological and behavioral characteristics of various stages of spiritual growth may be mixed. The most obvious characteristics indicate the dominant state of consciousness.

First Stage: Semiconscious Awareness

Related to the first chakra at the base of the spine.

- Mental dullness, apathy, or boredom are common.
- Intellectual powers are limited.
- Understanding of spiritual realities is minimal or absent.
- If one is religious, prayer may be directed to an erroneous concept of God.
- The soul may be considered as what one "has" rather than what one is.
- Activities, goals, and relationships are primarily motivated by needs related to physical well-being, desires, or whims.
- Habits, subconscious conditionings, irrational thinking, and inclinations to conform to the behaviors and expectations of others usually determine behaviors and lifestyle choices.
- Provincialism (small-mindedness) is common.
- Awareness is blurred and fragmented.
- Insecurity, fear, and uncertainty may be dramatized.
- Illusions and delusions prevail.
- Anger or other symptoms of frustration may be expressed when

needs or desires are not easily or quickly satisfied.

Children may express some of the last three characteristics when endeavoring to adapt to their environment or when confronted by unfamiliar events or circumstances.

Second Stage: Dysfunctional Self-Consciousness

Related to the sacral chakra, lower back.

• Conflicted mental and emotional states are common.
• Egocentricity prevails.
• Meditation may be practiced in the hope that peace of mind and spiritual growth may result.
• One may tend to be fascinated by or preoccupied with psychic phenomena, channeling (mediumship), and other practices which are spiritually useless.
• Illusions, emotional attachments, addictions, dependency, and self-defeating behaviors are common.
• Thinking may be irrational and behaviors unpredictable.
• Neurotic needs, a tendency to compare oneself with others and to feel that others are more fortunate, envy, jealously, emotional instability, moodiness, irresponsible behaviors, blaming others or circumstances, resistance to conform to ideal or appropriate behaviors, mental perversity, and fantasies are common.
• Subconscious influences dominate mental and emotional states.
• Behaviors may include attempts to reach out, to "touch" the environment to experience and relate to it.
• Sensuality, confusion, indecision, unregulated imagination, role playing, and pretending to be the hero or heroine of one's fantasies are common.

Adolescents may have some of these characteristics when still learning to relate to the world.

Third Stage: Functional Self-consciousness

Related to the lumbar chakra opposite the navel.

- A somewhat healthy-minded but still egocentric state.
- If one meditates, the primary purpose may be to only elicit relaxation, manage stress, and derive psychological and physical benefits.
- Thinking is orderly and rational. Behaviors are wholesome and purposeful.
- Relationships are meaningful and supportive. Actions are skillful and goals can be easily achieved.
- Partial intellectual understanding of one's true nature and of God may be present.
- One may be interested in acquiring an understanding of metaphysical principles that can provide insight into higher realities and the subjective causes of events and circumstances.
- A dominant sense of personality-oriented self-identity may incline one to want to demonstrate personal power, be in control, attain recognition, and accomplish goals.
- Unbounded optimism may prevail along with thoughts and feelings that anything is possible.

Young adults may have some of these characteristics when they become independent and endeavor to relate to the world on their terms. Emotionally mature individuals awakening from this stage who sincerely desire to actualize their innate potential are ready for discipleship.

Fourth Stage: Superconsciousness

Related to the dorsal chakra between the shoulder blades.

- Knowledge that one is a unit of God's being.
- Superconscious states are easily experienced which allow perceptions of transcendent realities.
- Ego-sense is diminished as Self-realization blossoms.

- Activities are chosen and relationships are entered into and experienced without compulsion.
- Aspiration to be fully awake is usually pronounced.
- Lifestyle changes may spontaneously occur, or be chosen.
- Desire for soul happiness is fervent.

Adults may express some of these characteristics during their middle years because of having experienced lifestyle changes and impermanent relationships and because of a sincere desire to live a more meaningful life.

Fifth Stage: Cosmic Consciousness

Related to the cervical chakra opposite the throat.

- Partial apprehension of cosmic processes and knowledge that the universe is a play of cosmic forces.
- Perceptions are insightful and accurate.
- The constituent attributes of Primordial Nature (Om, space, time, and cosmic forces) are easily comprehended.
- Activities and relationships are enjoyable.
- Because of fervent aspiration to spiritual growth and knowing that physical life is temporary, behaviors may be more focused on acquiring valid knowledge and to growing to emotional and spiritual maturity.

People near retirement age often express some of these characteristics as they withdraw from former responsibilities and more seriously contemplate the meaning of life and the inevitability of their eventual transition from the body.

Sixth Stage: God-Consciousness

Related to the spiritual eye center between the eyebrows and the front lobes of the brain.

- Clear Self and God-awareness.
- If karmic conditions are influential, they are easily resisted,

weakened, and rapidly removed by personal choice and by superior superconscious influences that prevail.
• Consistent right actions and God-awareness prevent the accumulation of troublesome subconscious conditionings.
• Emotional maturity and spiritual awareness are expressed as righteous, benevolent behaviors.

Seventh Stage: Spiritual Enlightenment

The crown chakra, related to the higher brain.

• Self- and God-realization prevails with intuitive knowledge of cosmic processes.
• When meditating, realizations are transcendent.
• When performing duties and observing transitory events, Self-knowledge, God-realization, and clear apprehension of the wholeness of life does not waver.
• Actions are spontaneously appropriate.
• Consciousness is liberated: without delusions or illusions. Karma is neutralized or transcended.
• One is inclined to perform appropriate, selfless service to assist others and society to the highest good.

How to Awaken From Where You
Are to Where You Want to Be

Aspire to the level of awareness you desire to experience. Mental and spiritual laws (principles that remain constant) of cause and effect, like catalysts that causes chemical changes to occur without themselves being changed, make possible the actualization of conditions we can imagine and believe to be true. Envisioned ideal states of awareness are not created; they are allowed to emerge.

Adopt mental attitudes, emotional states, and behaviors that are in accord with the stage of spiritual growth you want to prevail. If you think (or feel) that by doing this you are not being self-honest, your understanding of what you really are is deficient. Your pure-conscious Self is not the conditioned mental state of ordinary awareness. When you aspire to Self- and God-realization you are aspiring to awaken to the truth of your being. It is your destiny to be spiritually awake. Be firmly resolved to fulfill your destiny.

If thoughts, feelings, or desires that are inconsistent with your resolve to be spiritually awake arise, use will power to resist them, then replace them with constructive thoughts, feelings, and aspirations. Resolve to be self-responsible.

Your awareness expresses through your body and mind. Nurture physical health and psychological well-being until nothing exists that can interfere with your ability to perceive with accuracy and to function effectively.

Meditate daily to the stage of superconsciousness. When you are superconscious, your attention removed from distractions and limitations, your awareness is clear. After resting in this clear state for a while, contemplate your true nature and the reality of God. Avoid impatience. At the core of your being you are already free and knowledgeable. Allow necessary psychological and physiological changes to occur in the course of time.

Affirmation
I am fully committed to rapid awakening through
the remaining stages of spiritual growth.

When the constituent attributes of the universe and one's relationship to it are understood; and when it is understood that it is delusion alone that causes souls to forget their true nature and experience suffering, one naturally wishes to be relieved from all misfortune. Thus, liberation from the bondage of delusion becomes the primary aim of life.

– *Swami Sri Yukteswar*

FIVE

How to Make Your Life Worthwhile

We are not in this world to passively drift with the tides of ever-changing events, aggressively fulfill useless desires in a vain attempt to express limited personal powers, be preoccupied with indiscriminate or unregulated gratification of the senses, or imitate the behaviors of others whose lives are purposeless or misdirected. We are here for a higher purpose which, when discovered and fulfilled, provides permanent peace of mind and lasting soul fulfillment.

In this chapter I share what I have learned from personal experience and from others who are spiritually awake and wise. Use this information to make your life worthwhile. By diligent, right endeavor and with God's grace, you can do it.

There is a "Right Place" in the Universe for You

Actions do not bind the person who has renounced them ... whose doubts have been banished by knowledge, and who is permanently established in Self-realization. – *Bhagavad Gita 4:41*

The "right place" for you is where you are in relationship to the rhythms of life. You will then more easily experience the harmonious integration of the spiritual, mental, physical, and environmental aspects that comprise your existence. You will know that you are *there* when "your heart (being) sings with joy" and all of your circumstances and relationships, and the unplanned events that occur, are in "divine order."

Many people who are without a clear sense of meaningful purpose are suffering from a debilitating condition that used to be diagnosed as *neurasthenia*, a word used to cover a variety of symptoms: weariness, lack of energy, mental dullness and confusion, a prevailing feeling of inadequacy, and inability or reluctance to confront and effectively relate to everyday circumstances. These characteristics were once thought to be caused by nervous exhaustion. If no physical imbalance exists, the cause of the problem is usually self-centeredness along with thoughts and feelings of being separated from God, others, and supportive circumstances. This condition is easily cured by 1) renouncing or transcending egocentricity in favor of Self-knowledge and emotional maturity; 2) acquiring knowledge and functional skills to live effectively, and going forward with plans to fulfill meaningful purposes.

To live effectively:

• Study to learn about the reality of God, your true nature as a spiritual being, and the laws of cause and effect.
• Ask, from the core of your being, "What is my right place in life?" Don't ask anyone for their opinion about the matter. You alone know the answer. Inquire until it emerges from within you and is clear in your mind and awareness.
• Balance your life with regular practice of superconscious meditation and wholesome participation in activities which are of value to you and of benefit to others.

Experience the Redemptive Effects of Inspired
Imagination and Wisdom-Directed Actions

Ask, and it shall be given to you; seek, and you shall find; knock, and it shall be opened to you. – *The Gospel of Matthew 7:7*

Thoughts and imaginal states can produce corresponding effects. What kind of thoughts habitually pervade your mind? What mental pictures and expectations of near and future events and circumstances do you nurture and sustain? Are you always optimistic: do you look for and expect the best results in any situation? What are your normal behaviors? Are they life-enhancing and appropriate, or are they impelled by your subconscious conditionings or emotional reactions?

You, as a spiritual being, express through your mind and body. Your mind (and the mind of every person and creature) is a part of an omnipresent Cosmic Mind which is responsive to thoughts, mental concepts, and desires. Weak, disordered thoughts and mental concepts are impotent. Dominant, well-defined thoughts and mental concepts reinforced by faith (and constructive actions, when necessary) produce effects.

How we habitually think and behave is determined by our states of consciousness. When we are spiritually aware, we are inclined to think rationally and to perform actions that produce desired results. When we are not spiritually aware, we are inclined to be illusional, and do not know (or pretend not to know) the relationships between causes and effects, our thinking tends to be confused, purposes are unclear, and behaviors are erratic or self-defeating.

Armed with knowledge of your true nature in relationship to the wholeness of life, discipline yourself to think rationally, use your powers of imagination creatively for constructive purposes, and act wisely and decisively. You have the same potential to be Self-realized and functionally effective as every other soul. The laws of cause and effect are universal and impersonal. Rather than try to "use" the laws, cooperate with them by adapting your thinking and behaviors to them.

If you have needs (for healing, peace of mind, improved relationships, prosperity), first cultivate spiritual awareness. When you are spiritually aware and your thinking is rational you will know what to do to help yourself and all of the conditions you consider to be ideal will naturally unfold.

It is, of course, useful to think constructively and use your powers of imagination before you are fully, spiritually awake. Imagine what is true of you as a spiritual being: *see* and *feel* yourself in the wholeness of the infinite (endless) ocean of Consciousness in which you and all things now exist. Established in this awareness of what is true, thoughts or feelings of lack or limitation do not exist.

When imagining ideal circumstances—for spiritual growth,

overall well-being, the accomplishment of purposes, or the fulfillment of desires—assume (adopt) the mental attitude and outlook, state of awareness, and feelings that you will have when what you imagine is actual. If this is not done, there will be a gap between you and the desired outcome. Endeavors to use positive thinking, visualization, affirmations, prayer, or any other goal-achievement methods to fulfill desires or accomplish purposes without assuming the mental state, state of awareness, and feeling of fulfillment will be in vain, or the results will be incomplete or unsatisfying. This is why many truth seekers are not able to have positive results—they try to "make something happen" but are not able (or willing) to experience the necessary shift of viewpoint and awareness that would allow the desired results to occur. They are fixated or stuck in their belief and feeling of lack while hoping for improvement or change.

Discover Anew the Nurturing
Power of Compassion

To practice [these] five things everywhere constitutes perfect virtue: dignified conduct based on good character, generosity of soul, sincerity, purposeful intention, and kindness. *– Attributed to Confucius*

It is not only for ourselves that we cultivate our innate qualities and are dedicated to making our lives worthwhile. As we become more conscious and capable, our clear states of awareness and constructive behaviors benefit all others with whom we share a common origin and destiny. While we are growing in knowledge and wisdom we should do what we can to assist others to their highest good. Although we cannot control (nor should we desire to do so) what others do, we can silently love and bless them, pray for their well-being and spiritual growth, personally encourage and assist them when possible, and inspire them with our own appropriate, God-centered behavior. The nurturing power of compassion blesses equally the one who expresses it and those who are lovingly cared for.

Knowledge That Liberates

Focus your attention within. You will experience new power, new strength, and new peace of body, mind, and spirit. Then all bonds that limit you will be removed. – *Paramahansa Yogananda*

The following kinds of knowledge remove all limitations:

1. *Self-realization, perception and experience of the essence of being.* Accomplished by intellectual and intuitive Self-analysis and skillful, superconscious meditation practice supported by wholesome, purposeful, effective living.
2. *God-realization, direct experience of the totality of the field of infinite Consciousness.* It occurs naturally when Self-realization is refined.
3. *Knowledge of the origins and processes of the universe.* It is then understood that the universe emanates from a field of Primordial Nature which is manifested and sustained by the power of Consciousness.
4. *Knowledge of the laws of cause and effect.* We can then know why circumstances are as they are and how they can be improved or changed.
5. *Knowledge of how to live effectively.*

In early stages of inquiry, information that is acquired may not be fully comprehended. When understanding dawns, you will have knowledge. When your knowledge has replaced erroneous concepts and illusions, you will have wisdom.

Affirmation
Inspired and soul-motivated, I wisely use my knowledge and abilities to make my life worthwhile and to benefit others.

The Masters say that the soul has two faces. The higher one always sees God, the lower one looks downward and informs the senses. The higher one is the summit of the soul, it gazes into eternity.
– *Meister Eckhart (1260 – 1327)*

SIX

Exploring Transcendental States of Consciousness

Even when we are healthy, reasonably happy, and personal circumstances provide comfort and security, until we are spiritually enlightened, we cannot be completely peaceful. A prevailing sense of "divine discontent" impels us to want to see beyond our limitations—to no longer be confined to ordinary states of awareness which obscure perceptions of a higher reality we intuitively know exists and is accessible.

Fleeting episodes of transcendence (rising above, passing over, or going beyond ordinary boundaries of thinking, states of awareness, or perception) have been reported by millions of people, most of whom were surprised by the suddenness of the event and were not able to elicit a similar experience. Some individuals who are familiar with meditative techniques or who have exceptional powers of concentration can assume a clarified state of consciousness at will.

Of his transcendental perceptions, Albert Einstein wrote:

It is very difficult to explain this feeling to anyone who is entirely without it, especially as there is no anthropomorphic [humanlike] conception of God corresponding to it. The individual feels the nothingness of human desires and aims and the sublimity and marvelous order which reveal themselves both in Nature and in the world of thought. He looks upon individual existence as a sort of prison and wants to experience the universe as a single significant whole.

Edwin Schrodinger, a scientist who explored the field of quantum mechanics (the study of the structure and behavior of atoms and molecules), said:

Inconceivable as it seems to ordinary reason, you—and all other conscious beings—are all in all. Hence, this life of yours … is not merely a piece of the entire existence, but is in a certain sense the whole.

In regard to prayer in relationship to transcendental states, a Hebrew mystic, Rabbin Eleazar, wrote:

Think of yourself as nothing and totally forget yourself when you pray. Only remember that you are praying for the Divine Presence. You may then enter the Universe of Thought, a state of consciousness which is beyond time. Everything in this realm is the same … [perceived as oneness] but in order to enter this realm you must relinquish your ego and forget your troubles.

The 16th century Spanish mystic John Yepes (St. John of the Cross), wrote about his transcendental experiences. Note the following account of a profound event that occurred during his early thirties when, feeling desolate, he sought the solution to his problem while absorbed in intensive prayerful contemplation:

After some time, certain rays of light, comfort and divine sweetness scattered these mists and translated the soul of the servant of God into a paradise of interior delights and heavenly sweetness. This sovereign wisdom is of an excellence so high that no faculty nor science can unto it attain.

Of this and other episodes, he wrote:

This is nothing else but the supernatural light giving light to the understanding, so that human understanding becomes divine, made one with the divine.

In the classic text *Vasishta Yoga* (India, circa 2000 B.C.E.), the author has a character describe the experience of freedom that can result when one's awareness is clarified by superconscious realization:

I was long enslaved by the great enemy, ignorance, which robbed me of my wealth of wisdom. But now, by God's grace and my own excellent self-endeavor, I have attained wisdom. By Self-knowledge the shadow of ego-sense has been removed. Rid of the poverty of delusion, I remain supremely free. All that is worth knowing is known. All that is worth seeing has been seen. I have attained that beyond which there is nothing to be attained.

The following, interesting account told by an anonymous woman in the latter part of the 19th century is included in the book *Cosmic Consciousness* by Richard Maurice Bucke, M.D. (first published in 1901):

Perfect rest and peace and joy were everywhere, and, more strange than all, there came to me a sense as of some serene, magnetic *presence*—grand and pervading. Presently what seemed to be a swift, oncoming tidal wave of splendor and glory ineffable came down upon me, and I felt myself enveloped, swallowed up. ... I was losing my consciousness, my identity, but was powerless to hold myself. Now came a period of rapture, so intense that the universe stood still, as if amazed by the unutterable majesty of the spectacle! One in all the infinite universe! The All-Loving, the Perfect One! The Perfect Wisdom, truth, love, and purity! And with the rapture came the insight. In that same wonderful moment of what might be called supernal bliss, came illumination. I saw with intense inward vision the atoms or molecules, of which seemingly the universe is composed—I know not whether material or spiritual—rearranging themselves, as the cosmos (in its continuous, everlasting life) passes from order to order. What joy when I saw there was no break in the chain—not a link left out—everything in its place and time. Worlds, systems, all blended in one harmonious whole. Universal life, synonymous with universal love!

The German philosopher Matwilda von Meysenburg used these words to describe a spontaneous experience:

I was alone upon the seashore ... I felt that I returned from the solitude of individuation into the consciousness of unity with all that is... earth, heaven, and sea resounded in one vast world encircling harmony ... I felt myself one with them.

After praying for an hour, a contemporary Franciscan nun reported:

I felt communion, peace, an openness to experience ... [and] an awareness and response to God's presence around me ... centering, quieting, nothingness ... moments of fullness of the presence of God permeating my being.

Several years after having his first experience in cosmic consciousness my guru, Paramahansa Yogananda, described the revelation in a poem. In this excerpt, the word *samadhi* is used to indicate his vivid perception of "wholeness."

Knowing, knower, Known, as One!
Tranquilled, unbroken thrill, eternally living,
   ever-new peace.
Enjoyable beyond imagination of expectancy,
   samadhi bliss!
Not an unconscious state
Or mental chloroform without willful return,
Samadhi but extends my conscious realm
Beyond the limits of the mortal frame
To farthest boundary of eternity
Where I, the Cosmic Sea,
Watch the little ego floating in Me.

After such episodes, most people say they saw the order, harmony, and goodness of life; were inspired to live with a renewed sense of purpose; and no longer feared death. They did not feel superior or special; they felt humble. They also say that everyone can experience transcendence.

Some individuals report having only one such experience. Others, knowing how to calm the mind and make themselves receptive, were able to have similar experiences that enlarged their understanding and enabled them to integrate their realizations into their everyday lives.

Science Examines Subjective States of Consciousness

Neurotheology (neuro: nerve; theology, the study of God and religious experience) is a word used by researchers attempting to discover what occurs in the nervous system and brain when a person perceives a reality different from and more meaningful than what is ordinarily experienced. Data they obtain from meditators and persons who prayed enables them to relate subjective states of awareness to specific regions of the brain.

The prefrontal region of the brain is active when attention is concentrated. This is one reason why persons who practice forms of yoga meditation are advised to direct their attention to the upper forehead when meditating.

The area toward the top and back of the brain has been named the "orientation association area" because it processes information about space and time and the orientation of the body in space. It helps us to determine where the body ends and the external environment begins. If sensory input is blocked to this region, the brain is prevented from forming a distinction between "self" and "nonself." When the left orientation area cannot then find any boundary between the self and the world, the self is perceived as being one with everything. When the right orientation area is quiet, one may feel that only infinite space exists.

Experiments, during which a weak magnetic field is placed near the left side of the brain, have caused volunteer subjects to experience a sensation of a "presence" often described as divine or benevolent, or a seeming out-of-body sensation. Sensory deprivation, lack of oxygen, extreme tiredness, and participation in ritual behaviors (such as rhythmic dancing, drumming, running, singing, chanting, and religious rites) can also cause altered states of consciousness. A severe personal crisis may also contribute to such experiences.

Because some "spiritual experiences" may be associated with specific neural stimulation (or lack of it), it should not be too quickly presumed that all such episodes are brain-produced illusions. It may be that in some instances the stimulation or quieting of various areas of the brain "allows" transcendental feelings and insights to be perceived rather than being their cause.

Authentic spiritual perceptions and the emergence of innate knowledge in regard to one's real nature and relationship to the Infinite always contribute to healthy-mindedness, a diminishing of egotism, and a keen interest in life and living. Disordered mental and emotional states and or hallucinations may result in confusion, an exaggerated sense of self-importance, or lack of interest in living.

The nervous system coordinates and regulates internal functions of the body and responses to external stimuli. It consists of the brain, spinal cord, nerves, and ganglia (nerve cells outside the brain and spinal cord) and comprises the sympathetic and parasympathetic nervous systems.

The sympathetic nervous system tends to depress secretions, decrease smooth muscle tone and contract vascular systems (vessels through which fluids circulate). It regulates physical characteristics associated with arousal and action—the "flight or fight response" related to survival behaviors.

The parasympathetic nervous system, originating in the central and back parts of the brain and lower part of the spinal cord, regulates the digestive system, slows the heart, dilates blood vessels, and has a quieting influence.

The brain, which weighs about three and a half pounds in an adult person, is the part of the central nervous system that interprets sensory impulses, coordinates and regulates bodily functions, and processes awareness, thoughts, and emotions.

A person who does not comprehend the reality of God may be inclined to assert that the brain produces the mind. A more insightful person will say the brain is the organ of the mind which is other than and superior to the brain. And other than and superior to the mind is the true Self which uses the mind, brain, and body.

How to Prepare Yourself to Explore
Transcendental States of Consciousness

Although it is possible that a transcendental episode can occur suddenly without prior indication, when one is prepared to experience it, it will be easier to recognize and be easier to have similar experiences.

To be receptive to experiencing clear states of awareness:

• Aspire to Self- and God-realization. Think about the possibility. Be confident that because you are a spiritual being it is your destiny to be fully awake to the truth of what you are and your relationship to the Infinite.

• Live a wholesome, balanced, purposeful, uncomplicated life with conscious intention. Doing this will contribute to physical and psychological health, enable you to avoid misfortune, and allow spiritual growth to unfold naturally.

• Cultivate attributes which are characteristic of enlightened consciousness: contentment; rational thinking and emotional stability; optimism; enthusiasm; cheerfulness; compassion; creativity; appropriate, ethical behavior; self-discipline and mastery of attention; and a keen interest in further learning and spiritual growth.

• Improve and use your powers of discriminative intelligence and intuition. Learn to discern the difference between your essence of being and ordinary states of awareness.

• Improve your understanding of God, your true nature, and your relationship to your mind and body and the world.

• Grow to emotional maturity; be responsible for your thoughts, feelings, and behaviors.

• Renounce erroneous ideas and opinions.

• Purify the ego (illusional sense of selfhood). A distinct sense of individuality enables us to relate to the world and to others. It can be perceived as what it is—an assumed point of view from which we observe events and circumstances while knowing that we are units of a larger field of reality.

How to Be Receptive to Realizing
Higher States of Consciousness

Transcendental (superconscious) perceptions are easier to have when the mind is calm and the nervous system is refined.

• Meditate on a regular schedule to internalize your attention and experience superconscious states. When meditating, focus your awareness in the front and upper region of the brain. If you use a meditation technique, when your mind and awareness are calm and clear, disregard the technique. Rest in the silence, alert and attentive. Contemplate wholeness.

  Before experiencing wholeness, you may feel as though you are communing with a larger field of reality. When transcendence occurs and the act of meditating ceases, you will experience pure, infinite being. By repeated practice, you will learn to maintain your inward awareness of wholeness at all times after meditating.

  When meditating, concentration may be interrupted by emotions and thoughts driven by impulses arising from the unconscious. Ignore them and they will soon subside. Patterns of light, visions of various kinds, or ecstatic feelings may occasionally be perceived. Observe them with dispassionate objectivity and go beyond them. Whatever you perceive that is subject to change is not the final state you aspire to realize.

• When you are not meditating, keep your awareness in the three higher vital centers (chakras) in your spine and head (the dorsal and cervical centers and the spiritual eye in the forehead. This practice will encourage your vital forces to flow upward and enable you to be more conscious, alert, attentive, and insightful while performing your duties. It will also nurture the further development of the front lobes of your brain which are related to optimism, creativity, concentration, will power, and self-control.

Superconscious states may also be experienced when one is

in the presence of an enlightened person or when such a person assists others with prayer or transmits spiritual force to them. This force can awaken the dormant energies of a receptive person, somewhat clarify their awareness, and allow them a glimpse of higher realities. The effects of such transmission are determined by one's degree of receptivity.

A fleeting transcendental experience is only the beginning for a spiritual aspirant who is dedicated to God-realization. When one knows that higher realities exist and are accessible, a commitment must be made to the path of discipleship (learning and disciplined living) that can result in psychological transformation and nurturing and actualization of innate soul qualities. We can help ourselves to spiritual growth and liberation of consciousness by removing the mental and physical obstacles that blur and confine our awareness. When we sincerely do our utmost to help ourselves by right thinking and living and right spiritual enquiry, the supportive, redemptive impulses of grace can more easily assist us to our highest good.

Right spiritual enquiry is that approach to Self-discovery and God-knowledge which enables us to live effectively, be skillfully proficient in superconscious meditation practice, and experience rapid, authentic spiritual growth. Progress is slow, moderate, or fast in accord with our concentrated endeavors.

Some individuals are satisfied with only mild improvement that enables them to live comfortably. Others want the benefits of enlightened consciousness while retaining self-centered attitudes and behaviors. A few fervently yearn to be fully, spiritually awake and are willing to undergo the psychological (and sometimes, lifestyle) changes which may be necessary for them.

Superconsciousness is as different from ordinary states of awareness as ordinary states are from unconsciousness. People whose awareness is ordinary are usually confused. Their powers of concentration are weak. Their awareness is fragmented. Delusions and illusions prevail. Negative mental attitudes and addictive or habit-driven behaviors incline them to wander aimlessly in space and time as though in a dream. All souls have the same innate qualities. All souls can (and eventually will) fully awaken to Self- and God-realization.

Affirmation
Now having knowledge of higher realities and
my potential for spiritual fulfillment, I joyfully and
diligently do all that I can to be receptive to that
which is possible for me to realize.

We live in succession, in division, in parts, in particles. Meantime within ... is the soul of the whole; the wise silence; the universal beauty, to which every part and particle is equally related; the eternal One. And this deep power in which we exist and whose beatitude is all accessible to us, is not only self-sufficing and perfect in every hour, but the act of seeing and the thing seen, the seer and the spectacle, the subject and the object, are one. – *Ralph Waldo Emerson (1803 – 1882)*

SEVEN

Liberation of Consciousness: The Ultimate Purpose of Your Life

A firm belief in the possibility of deliverance from suffering, misfortune, and limitation is the base from which many of the world's religious movements and teachings have emerged. Those which emerged because of the enlightenment of the founders also tend to emphasize that awakening to a clear state of awareness removes one from the unhappiness and misfortune commonly experienced by people whose states of awareness are ordinary.

"Ordinary" awareness, blurred by modified mental states and an illusional sense of self-identity, is the normal condition for most people. That is why it is so difficult for them to comprehend a higher order of reality and to learn and do what is necessary to experience satisfying spiritual growth.

Spiritually unenlightened people mistakenly perceive themselves as physical beings. If they are materialistic they may believe that their mind, intellect, consciousness, and sense of self-identity is produced by their brain. Because their awareness is fragmented and restricted, their primary concern is to have and maintain a comfortable human existence rather than aspire to authentic spiritual growth that would allow their innate qualities to be unveiled and actualized. Although comfortable existence that provides human happiness and personal freedom is of value, it cannot completely satisfy because our innate urge is to be Self- and God-realized.

The *Self* to be realized is the essence of our being. That which we refer to as God is the one field of Consciousness in which space-time phenomena exists and is individualized and expressive as you, me, and all other units of Consciousness in this and all other realms.

If knowledge of Consciousness is within us, why is it not always obvious? When we are not aware of the knowledge, capacities, qualities, and functional abilities that we innately have, it is because delusions and illusions obscure the truth. The solution to the problem of spiritual ignorance (lack of higher knowledge) is to purify the mind and ego, refine the brain and nervous system, and clarify awareness.

* When the mind is no longer confused or disordered, rational thinking is possible.
* When the ego is purified and is, therefore, healthy, we perceive ourselves to be units of infinite Consciousness.
* When the brain and nervous system are refined, we have exceptional intellectual and intuitive powers and functional abilities.
* When awareness is clarified, we are established in Self-knowledge. Cosmic conscious states and God-realization then spontaneously emerge.

One who sincerely desires to awaken to Self- and God-realization must be willing to make a radical adjustment in mental attitude, outlook, and behavior to go to the core of the matter. To do this, it is necessary to think rationally, be optimistic about the outcome of endeavors to nurture spiritual growth, and act constructively. To merely hope to awaken through the stages of spiritual growth while allowing the mind to be disordered, pessimism to prevail, and behaviors to be dictated by random moods or harmful habits, is useless. Mastery of attention cannot be acquired without self-control and self-discipline. A negative mental attitude distorts perceptions and makes it difficult for us to see opportunities that would allow us to experience good fortune. Moodiness and harmful habits blur awareness, confine us to ordinary states of awareness, and invite misfortune.

Liberation is *salvation* (Latin *salvātiō*; Greek *soteria*). The early Christian meaning of salvation was deliverance from faulty living and admission into a condition of eternal bliss. In our current era, this ideal condition is widely understood to be possible for any spiritual aspirant to realize regardless of a formal religious affiliation or lack of it.

In some liberation teachings the idea of human weakness that requires divine intervention is emphasized. Others assert that liberation may be accomplished by actualizing the soul's powers of will and its capacities to reason, meditate, nurture compassion, and choose ethical and moral behaviors. The overcoming of subconscious conditionings by eliminating mental and physical obstacles to the soul's urge to have its awareness restored to wholeness "allows" liberation to be spontaneously realized.

People who think themselves to be helpless may tend to look to a savior-figure or avatar (incarnation of God) who, it is hoped, will rescue them from their unfortunate condition and restore them to wholeness. While many enlightened men and women are now on earth, neither their presence nor their wise words or inspired actions can be redemptive unless those who are in need are mentally and spiritually receptive.

I am occasionally informed by well-meaning individuals that they have heard of, or met, an avatar or that someone has prophesied that one will soon emerge to establish a peaceful world order and ensure the well-being of all people. The only permanent solution to the problem of human suffering is for each individual to awaken from ordinary, conditioned states of awareness. Acknowledging the enlightenment of others who are fully awake can inspire us; only our own enlightenment can liberate us.

Liberation is of two kinds:

1. *Limited.* At this stage, one may be spiritually awake and functional enough to enjoy good fortune and be healthy, and again experience misfortune or ill health when attention is distracted, awareness is blurred, or mental confusion occurs. With limited liberation one is "free while embodied" so long as awareness remains clear. When awareness is not clear, subconscious conditionings may be influential or subliminal tendencies may cause the mind to be restless or disturbed.

2. *Absolute.* Permanent freedom from all limiting conditions. At this stage one is supremely liberated, with no possibility of a return to former, conditioned states.

Decide Now to Be Liberated as Soon as Possible

Think of liberation of your consciousness as being possible in this incarnation rather than as a condition to attain when you depart from this world. Many "truth students" are not unlike adherents of some traditional religious groups; they think of liberation of consciousness as a possible after-death event. The factors that contribute to this way of thinking vary:

* Erroneous, traditional ideas acquired many years ago may influence thoughts and behaviors.
* Frequent association with others who talk about and live in accord with their erroneous beliefs may reinforce the habit of irrational thinking.
* Preoccupation with, or being easily distracted by, matters of lesser importance may cause one to think that enlightenment can be delayed until their retirement years (or other favorable circumstances) allow them more time to nurture spiritual growth.
* The most common causes are a lack of sincere desire to be liberated and complacency: smug, self-centered satisfaction with existing conditions.

Someone may say, "I sincerely desire to be liberated," yet their everyday words and behaviors may not conform to their assertion. Or, "I am not satisfied with my existing conditions," yet do very little to improve them.

Among the last words my guru Paramahansa Yogananda said to me, during a private conversation in 1952, were: "Don't look back. Don't look to the right or to the left. Go all the way [to liberation consciousness in this lifetime]. You can!"

Aspire to be spiritually awake. Let your yearning to have your awareness completely restored to wholeness determine all of your thoughts, feelings, and actions.

• Avoid preoccupation with circumstances and relationships which are of little or no value. Decide how much time and energy to devote to metaphysical study, reading of secular newspapers and magazines or watching television to be informed of current events, meditation, work, your self-care and health routines, recreation, and social activity.
• Avoid allowing your attention to be distracted by focusing on worthy purposes and cultivating powers of concentration. Never think or say that you are helpless or cannot achieve your goals or accomplish your purposes. Every day, meditate until your mind is calm and your awareness is clear. Think rationally rather than allow emotions to dominate your thinking and behaviors. Nurture physical and psychological health.

Adhere to Wholesome Lifestyle Regimens

Spiritual growth cannot easily occur when the body is deprived of needed sleep or is undernourished or stressed. Psychological disorders and addictive behaviors also interfere with spiritual growth.

• Obtain sufficient sleep on a regular schedule. Allow thirty minutes or an hour for early morning spiritual practice and inspirational reading.
• Select a well-balanced, low-calorie, nutrition-rich diet. A vegetarian diet is healthier. Avoid fanaticism.
• Avoid stress by obtaining sufficient rest and exercise, wise management of time and personal resources, dispassionate (unemotional) observation of events and circumstances, and regular meditation practice.
• For psychological health, cultivate rational thinking. Avoid worry and thoughts and feelings of jealousy, envy, fear, grief, or guilt. Live a well-ordered life. Don't be concerned with what others think about you and don't compare yourself with others. Replace arrogance with humility. Be Self-content in

all circumstances, happy, and purposeful.
• Replace negative thoughts, feelings, and behaviors with constructive thoughts, feelings, and behaviors. Actualize your divine qualities.

Be Attentive to Useful Spiritual Practices

Spiritual practices include everything that can be done to nurture Self- and God-awareness. Complete spiritual practice consists of self-control, metaphysical study to acquire insight into higher realities, meditative contemplation, and surrender of the illusional sense of selfhood that allows the true Self and the reality of God to be experienced.

Avoid thinking that you do not have time or opportunities for spiritual practice. Every moment, regardless of where you are or what you are doing:

• Be aware of your true Self.
• Know that you now live in, and are one with, the wholeness of infinite Consciousness.
• Remember that Cosmic Mind is responsive to your mental states and thoughts and that the impulses of grace within and around you are supportive of you.
• Schedule a time for daily superconscious meditation. Write your practice routine. Consider your meditation session as an appointment with God, and faithfully keep that appointment. Your ultimate aim is liberation; do what is necessary to accomplish it.

Avoid the idea that your spiritual and secular (this world) life must be separate. The realm of nature is an interaction of cosmic forces emanated from one field of Consciousness. One of the most useful spiritual practices is to live so that all of your thoughts, actions, circumstances, and relationships are wholesome, constructive, and life-enhancing. Habits, subconscious conditionings, and genetic characteristics may be influential and have to be overcome. Unplanned events that distract your attention may occur. If you persist on your chosen spiritual path, you will eventually overcome or transcend all difficulties, awaken to Self- and God-realization, and fulfill your spiritual destiny.

Meditate With Conscious Intention

Passive meditation practice is of little value except for the relaxation that is experienced. When you start to meditate, be aware of the purpose of practice, which is to calm the mind and clarify your awareness so that you can experience your true nature as pure consciousness.

Don't practice meditation merely to create a pleasant mood or to produce visual or auditory phenomena. Go beyond all transitory perceptions to clear awareness of being. When the mind is calm and attention is focused, the reality of your real nature will shine of its own accord and knowledge of God that is innate to you will emerge.

Let Liberation Spontaneously Occur

Attentive, right spiritual practice will remove all obstacles to the natural emergence of your divine qualities. Rather than try to force enlightenment to occur, let it happen. At the innermost level of your being you are already whole, serene, and knowledgeable. It is only at the surface of your awareness that confusion can exist. When confusion and restlessness no longer prevail, distractions are avoided, and awareness remains clear, delusions and illusions cannot exist.

Provide a stable foundation for your life by having a clear sense of purpose and responsibly attending to your duties.

Cultivate harmlessness, honesty, and truthfulness. Avoid thoughts, emotions, and activities which needlessly waste your vital forces. While appropriately relating to the world, avoid strong mental or emotional attachments. You will then be "in the world but not of it." You will peacefully and effectively dwell here without being adversely influenced by anything.

Keep your mind and body pure. Be inwardly serene. Grow to

emotional maturity. Continue to learn. Be receptive to the blessings that life provides for you. Be kind to others, living things,
and the planet. Be thankful that you have knowledge of your
relationship to the Infinite and that your liberation is assured.
Let your light shine.

Affirmation
I am firmly resolved to be liberated in this incarnation.
After doing all that I can to nurture my spiritual growth,
I rest in the Infinite and let enlightenment emerge.
I am peaceful, happy, and receptive to my highest good.

I saw into that which was without end, things which cannot be uttered,
and of the greatness and infinitude... of God which cannot be expressed
by words. – *George Fox (1624 – 1691)*

EIGHT

How to Pray Effectively

Prayer is the opening of the heart (essence of being) to God. Two common prayer practices are 1) intimate dialogue or conversation and 2) communion with God, both of which indicate a presumption that God is other than or distinct (set apart) from the soul. Prayer that results in transcendental perception enables us to experience the reality of God.

Styles of prayer vary:

- Vocal: spoken aloud as a fixed or memorized form either reverently recited or spontaneously expressed.
- Mental: practiced silently.
- Contemplative: simple awareness of God's presence devoid of concepts or words.

Vocal prayer is usually easier to practice because it enables intention to be more easily focused. After a vocal prayer, the process can be mental, then contemplative. When prayer is vocal or mental, it is best to eventually stop "talking" and be silently aware of the reality of God.

Forms of prayer may be:

- Confessional: during which faults are honestly admitted, mental and spiritual renewal is experienced, and resolve to adopt ideal behaviors is made.
- Petitioning: asking for material or another kind of benefit.
- Intercessory: to assist others or to influence circumstances.
- Illuminating: for Self- and God-realization.

Confessional prayer enables one to think rationally about important matters, renounce arrogance in favor of humility, be inwardly refreshed, and commit to constructive action.

When praying for benefits—healing or improved well-being, guidance, prosperity, ideal relationships, or any other benefit— the key to effective prayer is to experience an obvious change of viewpoint and awareness, from feeling restricted or limited in any way to knowing that what is prayed for is already provided. *Then to live from that state of consciousness.*

To assist others or to influence circumstances, first pray to be aware of God's wholeness. Then think of others or of the circumstances that need to be improved and include them in your awareness of wholeness. There is no need to visualize a sequence of events that would result in answered prayer, or to mentally picture a specific outcome. God doesn't need to be told what to do or how to do it. Just rest in wholeness, knowing that the highest good will definitely emerge.

Researchers have discovered that prayer has influence. When hospitalized patients were prayed for, they rested better, had more peace of mind, and healed faster than patients who were not included on a prayer list. Individuals who knew they were on a prayer list improved more than individuals who, for the purpose of the study were not informed, perhaps because of knowing that they were being supported, and their own faith.

For illumination of consciousness, acknowledge your true nature as an immortal, spiritual being and that at the deepest level of your being you are already enlightened. Contemplate your true nature in relationship to the Infinite until thoughts cease and your awareness is clear, then rest in that state of mental and spiritual illumination. Maintain that realization after your interlude of meditative contemplation.

Whenever your attention becomes distracted, meditate to the stage of superconsciousness. In time, your awareness will always be clear, intellectual powers will be keen, intuition will be flawless, and perceptions will always be insightfully accurate.

Regardless of the style or form of your prayer practice, do it *in* God rather than pray *to* God. If you cannot at first be aware that you are always in God, pray any way that is meaningful to you, to any aspect of God which seems real to you. Continue until all sense of "otherness" dissolves.

If awareness of wholeness is not easily experienced, do not feel despair. Be patient. Pray and meditatively contemplate daily on a regular schedule. Faithfully and reverently doing this will not change God; it will change you.

Affirmation
As I pray and meditate in God, I am receptive to the good fortune that is mine to acknowledge and accept.

He who prays fervently knows not whether he prays ... for he is not thinking of the prayer he makes, but of God, to whom he makes it.
                                   – *Saint Francis of Sales (1567 – 1622)*

NINE

The Redemptive Power of Complete Dedication to the Spiritual Path

A spiritual path is a way of learning and living that will result in rapid spiritual growth—the progressive emergence of one's innate knowledge and qualities.

All sincere truth seekers who can think rationally and are willing to be self-disciplined and grow to emotional maturity can be successful on the spiritual path which is ideal for them. A meaningful spiritual path is not the way of naive belief in a philosophical doctrine or mechanical adherence to prescribed modes of behaviors.

An effective spiritual path is based on natural laws of cause and effect with practices adapted to the personal needs and psychological temperament of the individual. What is here recommended is suitable for all devotees on a spiritual path. These teachings are valid because they are reasonable and practical, and their usefulness has already been verified by others who have rightly used them.

The ultimate purpose of our lives is not what most people imagine.
– *Paramahansa Yogananda*

Our ignorance of higher realities and our dysfunctional behaviors must be honestly admitted to ourselves if we are to acquire useful knowledge, make wise choices, and experience the benefits of having done so. Religious scriptures describe this process of self-examination, followed by sincere intention to improve our circumstances, as repentance which makes possible the restoration of awareness to its original, unfragmented or pure condition.

We should ask: Why am I in this world? When it is clearly

understood that our real purpose for being here is to awaken from the semiconscious "dream" of mortality and be free of all limitations, we are inclined to 1) sincerely repent, 2) actively imagine possibilities for improvement, and 3) be inspired to do our utmost, with God's help, to fulfill our spiritual destiny.

Making a Commitment to the Spiritual Path

New wine must be put in new bottles ... – *The Gospel of Luke 5:38*

Some truth seekers want the benefits of spiritual practice without having to give up their habitual negative mental states or misguided behaviors. They want to be Self-realized while self-centered and cling to false concepts and opinions about God (because of sentiment, superstition, or lack of insight). Clarified states of awareness cannot be experienced when the mind is confused, erroneous ideas and illusions are dominant, and behaviors are allowed to be influenced by problem-causing subconscious conditionings or whims. The mind must be rational, the ego purified, the body refined, and behaviors well-ordered and constructive to allow spiritual growth to spontaneously occur. When obstacles to spiritual growth are removed, the luminosity and knowledge of the true Self emerges.

After choosing to be Self- and God-realized, it is necessary to be fully committed to a course of action that will allow the mind to be illumined and awareness to be enlightened. When we are thus resolved, much of the misfortune that might have occurred in the near or distant future is avoided because of constructive modes of thinking and behavior that are adopted. Also, superconscious influences that cleanse the subconscious are increasingly influential as spiritual growth progresses and receptivity to the influences of God's grace is greatly improved.

Living the Spiritual Path

Only the person who lives the [ideal] life will know the doctrine [the inner meaning of these teachings]. – *Words attributed to the Buddha*

One whose commitment to the spiritual path is complete will have little or no difficulty in doing what is necessary to accomplish the ultimate purpose of life.

• If knowledge about metaphysical (higher) realities and how to live effectively is needed, it will be acquired.
• Optimism, emotional stability, and skillful performance of duties will contribute to peace of mind, total well-being, and good fortune.
• Addictive tendencies will be easily overcome or renounced.
• Thinking, emotions, actions, and personal relationships will be life-enriching and spiritually elevating.
• Resources and supportive events and circumstances will be easily attracted or spontaneously provided.
• Meditation practice will be enjoyable, transformative, revealing, and liberating.

Progress on a spiritual path—whether slow, faster, or rapid— is determined by attentiveness to right endeavors and grace. Mild endeavor allows modest results. Endeavor that is more intentional allows quicker results. Endeavors conformed to complete commitment to the spiritual path allow rapid progress.

"God helps those who help themselves" is an axiom: a self-evident, factual statement. God is not a humanlike being, observing and waiting to see if we will help ourselves before grace will be allowed to flow. Impulses of grace are always present and are influential when and where they can be expressive.

In religious thought, grace (Latin *grātia*, good will, from *gratus*, pleasing) is considered as good fortune or assistance that is freely given. Attempts to invoke the impulses of grace are successful only to the extent that our actions and change in mental attitude or state of consciousness enable us to be receptive to them. Often, after we have done our best to help ourselves, an attitude of total surrender results in flows of grace that do for us what we could not do.

A devotee asked his teacher, "I pray for God's grace and for your grace." The teacher replied, "God's grace you have. My grace [good will] is unwavering. All that is needed now is your own grace [good will toward yourself and responsiveness to all available blessings]."

When engaged in contemplative meditation, when you are relaxed, calm, and have concentrated on your chosen object or ideal for a while, stop trying. Sit still, as an observer. Let your deep, inner urge to have your awareness illumined determine your meditative experience.

At other times, be alert to indications that unplanned good fortune is harmoniously regulating your personal affairs and providing you with supportive circumstances. Be thankful for the blessings that you have.

The one field of Consciousness in which we abide is whole. When it seems that a Larger Something is providing for us, it is really but providing for itself. We are not always aware of what is happening behind the scenes and how the processes occur. When all erroneous ideas and illusions about ourselves in relationship to the Infinite are permanently absent, we can clearly see and continuously experience wholeness.

Affirmation
Inspired and highly motivated, I am firmly resolved
to be completely committed to my spiritual path.

Like a flock of homesick cranes flying night and day back to their mountain nests, let all my life take its voyage to its eternal home in one salutation to thee. – *Rabindranath Tagore (1861 – 1941)*

TEN

The Essence of Mysticism

Only authentic mystical insight and experience can result in Self- and God-realization. Infinite Consciousness transcends material phenomena that occurs in space-time. Being other than matter, yet emanating and sustaining the material realms, the reality of God can only be known by nonmaterial means: not by the mind or intellect, but by intuition (the soul's capacity to know independent of the senses).

The average person's idea of what a mystic is, is inaccurate. A mystic is a person whose ego (personality-oriented sense of self-identity) has been sufficiently purified to enable intuition to provide direct, unmodified perception of the true nature of the soul in relationship to God. The ego of individuals whose subjective perceptions are mixed with visions, emotions, or ecstatic states which may be thought of as being characteristic of "religious experience" is not yet purified. If these symptoms occur while a meditator is experiencing soul-God communion, unification of awareness with the one field of Consciousness is flawed. One whose ultimate goal is complete, permanent Self- and God-realization should aspire to that end. Practices that effect psychological transformation, ego-purification, and the removal of erroneous opinions that arise because of illusions should be learned and diligently applied.

The published information about some "saintly" individuals, whose reported experiences, behaviors, and words seem to indicate a degree of spiritual advancement, sometimes also describe behaviors and ideas which indicate a deficiency of understanding and psychological imbalance. A spiritually mature, Self-realized, God-conscious person is fully alert, healthy-minded, has a balanced personality, and is able to live effectively. If powers of

reason and intellect are defective, emotions are unsettled or conflicted, perceptions are flawed, or if purposes cannot be easily
fulfilled, emotional and spiritual maturity has not yet been
accomplished.

In the Bhagavad Gita, it is declared that there is a timeless,
"secret" means by which the mind can be purified in accord with
natural law, is easy for a sincere spiritual aspirant to practice,
and leads to realization along with knowledge of one's true Self
and God. It is only "secret" in the sense that many people are
either not aware of it or, if they are, do not understand it or its
value. It is the way of right (moral, ethical, constructive) living;
removal of physical, mental, and emotional conditions that
interfere with spiritual growth; and meditation practice that
results in clarified, superconscious states.

- Right living should be considered as the basis of everything
  we do. If we do not live in the right way, or are unable to comprehend why it is important to do so, it is unlikely that we will
  be able to engage in practices which will result in psychological transformation and spiritual growth. If the importance of
  right living is not understood or is ignored, how can we learn
  of higher realities and be consistent in spiritual practice?
- Physical conditions that interfere with spiritual growth can
  be removed by nurturing total health and well-being. Debilitating conditionings can be resisted, restrained, and eliminated
  by choosing not to be influenced by them, rational thinking,
  and regular practice of superconscious meditation. Emotional
  maturity can be actualized by cultivating inner peace and
  rational, self-responsible behaviors.
- Meditation can be practiced by detaching awareness from
  environmental, physical, sensory and mental conditions and
  directing attention first to the higher brain centers and then
  to alert contemplation of one's pure-conscious nature and of
  the one field of Consciousness. During early superconscious
  stages, our awareness may be somewhat clarified, with
  thoughts and emotions still present. When a refined super-

conscious state prevails and thoughts and emotions are disregarded, aspiration to experience the reality of God prevails.

Soul-impulses that cause spiritual awakening are referred to as actions of God's grace. Because souls are units of God's being, no distinction is to be made between the soul and God.

Knowledge of realities beyond intellectual or sensory powers of perception can be intuitively apprehended before they are directly perceived. When Self-awareness is no longer confined by the mind, intellect, or senses, innate knowledge of infinite Consciousness and its processes is unveiled and revealed. The consciously or unconsciously assumed habit of thinking, feeling, and behaving as though we are mere mortal creatures rather than spiritual beings is the primary cause of lack of Self- and God-knowledge.

Knowledge that is ever within the "darkness" (the inertia of nature and the clouded awareness of the spiritually unawake soul) is not always comprehended. When our awareness is clarified, knowledge of our true nature and of Consciousness is easily comprehended.

Until our knowledge of Consciousness and its aspects and processes is fully unveiled, an intellectual understanding of higher realities is helpful as we awaken through the stages of spiritual growth. For this reason, a devotee of God is encouraged to carefully examine what enlightened people have said in regard to such matters. Because knowing the inner causes of events enables us to better understand the circumstances that result, the most helpful place to begin our inquiry is at the source.

Egocentric people cannot perceive or comprehend the field of primordial nature which produced and sustains the physical realm, nor can they perceive or comprehend the reality of God. To be able to perceive and know that which is not obvious when awareness is ordinary, erroneous ideas should be renounced and mental and emotional calmness should be nurtured. Then the intellect can be purified and awareness clarified so that the soul's exceptional powers of perception can be utilized to facilitate spiritual growth.

New insights and newly awakened spiritual awareness may soon become distorted if mixed with erroneous ideas and conditioned states of awareness. Even when our aspiration to spiritual growth is fervent and we have good intentions, it is difficult to live a well-ordered life if harmful habits and self-centered or irrational behaviors are allowed to persist. An ordinary or "normal" personality-centered lifestyle, with mental attitudes and behaviors determined by subconscious conditionings is incompatible with aspiration for spiritual growth.

The emergence of innate soul qualities occurs naturally when conditions which might obstruct the soul's urge to be knowledgeable and free are absent. Right living along with right spiritual practice removes obstacles to spiritual growth.

To be spiritually enlightened is to be fully conscious of your real nature and have comprehensive knowledge of Consciousness and its processes. If you are not yet spiritually enlightened, resolve to be enlightened. If you are somewhat enlightened, aspire to be fully awake. Do practical things to assist your innate urge to be enlightened:

- Live an orderly (systematic, with a minimum of disruption) life. Decide how much attention and time to devote to metaphysical study, meditation practice, domestic duties, work, service, recreation, social relationships and activities, and whatever else you consider to be of value. Define and establish your priorities: do the most important things first.
- Cultivate moral and ethical behaviors. Train yourself to do what is right and appropriate in all situations.
- Acknowledge debilitating mental attitudes, thoughts, feelings, or personal behaviors that you allow to persist. Replace them with constructive mental states and behaviors.
- Periodically examine your basic mind-body constitution. To restore or maintain it in a state of balance, live in harmony with nature, and meditate.
- Meditate every day to the stage of superconsciousness.

- Contemplate the knowledge of higher realities that you want to have and the clarified state of awareness to which you aspire.

Diligently endeavor to elicit innate knowledge of your real nature and to know God as God is rather than be content to believe what others have said about God. Even if what others have said is true, their knowledge cannot liberate you. Only your perceptions of what is true and your Self- and God-realization can illumine your consciousness.

What erroneous beliefs should you discard? What mental attitudes do you need to renounce? What mental attitudes do you need to cultivate? What behaviors do you need to replace with more constructive behaviors? What relationships do you need to either improve or terminate? Are you purposeful? Are all of your purposes meaningful (of real value)? Write a list of your major purposes in order of their importance.

Meditate daily. After practicing your meditation technique routine, sit in silence, alert and attentive. Then contemplate your real nature as pure consciousness and the reality of God. Expand your awareness. Assume a viewpoint of being knowledgeable and free in the unbounded field of infinite Consciousness. After meditation practice, retain your soul and God-centered state and clarity of awareness as you attend to your duties and appropriately and supportively interact with others.

Decide Now to be Self-Realized

Why is it that many people, who are capable of rational thinking and say they want to be Self-realized, are not yet conscious of their real nature? Is Self-realization difficult to accomplish? Is it God's will that we not be Self-realized "until the time is right"? Are some soul's destined to be spiritually awake while others must remain only partially conscious?

It is not difficult to be Self-realized, nor is it God's will that our spiritual awakening be delayed. People who are not yet spiritually awake do not consider Self-realization to be as important as other matters which attract their attention and with which they choose to be involved. They prefer to behave like habit-bound victims of circumstances rather than acknowledge themselves as spiritual beings "in the image and likeness of God."

A person may sincerely say, "I'm doing my best to live a good life and to think positive, meditate, and be Self-realized." Ordinary, self-conscious endeavors are often inadequate. Without a clear sense of ultimate purpose, decisiveness, and enthusiasm to keep attention focused, ordinary endeavors seldom produce desired results.

The interest of many people who think of themselves as being on the spiritual path is superficial. Their participation is feeble. They are not sincerely intent on exploring the depths of philosophical concepts, discovering and experiencing the reality of God, or being enlightened and liberated. Their mental attitudes are provincial (small, limited). Their words and behaviors reveal their emotional immaturity.

One who is not committed on a spiritual path will usually:

• Resist learning new concepts or have difficulty comprehending them.

• Be inclined to mental perversity (to distort what is learned and to adapt or conform it to personal views and purposes).

• Be unable to concentrate effectively and have difficulty in adhering to useful self-care regimens and spiritual practice routines.

It is easier to awaken to Self- and God-realization when we are healthy-minded, emotionally mature, and intellectually competent.

To allow Self-realization to more easily occur:

• Cultivate the habit of rational thinking. Be realistic; avoid fantasies and illusions.

• Cultivate emotional maturity. Be responsible for your thoughts, feelings, actions, and the circumstances and relationships that result from your actions and choices.

- Acquire accurate information about how to live effectively and diligently apply it. Acquire accurate information about God, your relationship to God and nature, and how to rapidly awaken through the stages of spiritual growth.
- Expand your awareness; cultivate universal and cosmic consciousness.
- Acknowledge that your ultimate purpose in life is to be permanently spiritually enlightened. Thoughts, moods, and actions will no longer be negatively influenced by habits.
- Decide to soon be Self- and God-realized. Think, feel, and live in accord with your decision.
- When you have discovered your spiritual path—the one that is right for you—adhere to it with faith demonstrated by practice. You will avoid intellectual confusion: what Paramahansa Yogananda referred to as "spiritual indigestion."

While there can be no guarantee that implementation of these guidelines will result in Self-realization within a few weeks or months, spiritual growth will occur much faster than otherwise. Self-realization is not an effect of a cause; it is your natural state to which you can awaken when mental and emotional obstacles that obscure it have been removed or transcended.

The means by which all obstacles to God-realization can be removed are systematically described in Patanjali's yoga-sutras. These effective procedures, practiced together, are given the name *kriya* (constructive action that results in) *yoga* (conscious awareness of being "unified" with infinite Consciousness). For one who is committed to the spiritual path, the procedures are easy to learn and enjoyable to practice. For one who is undecided, or "double-minded" (who wants to be Self-realized while, at the same time, wants to preserve self-centered attitudes and behaviors), they are not easy to learn and are difficult to practice.

When Self-realization is your dominant aim in life, your thoughts and actions will be more easily organized to allow it to be quickly actualized. As a hungry person yearns for food, as a thirsty person yearns for water, as a person deprived of air yearns for it above all else, fervently aspire to be Self- and God-realized as soon as possible.

Affirmation
I know that I abide in the infinite ocean of God's wholeness.

In mystical experience the soul is aware of God as a reality into which it flows or which flows into it, and at the same time is conscious that this indissoluble unity is a union of two—of itself and of God who transcends it. – *Simon L. Frank (1877 – 1950)*

ELEVEN

Righteous Living as Spiritual Practice

Seek first to know the wholeness of God, and live righteously, and all
these things [whatever is needed] will be provided for you.
— *The Gospel of Matthew 6:36*

Concentrated spiritual practice allows our divine qualities and
to emerge more easily and quickly. Because most of our time and
attention is usually devoted to duties and to nurturing relationships, it is best to adopt right living as our primary spiritual
practice—supplemented with astute study of metaphysical principles and regular superconscious meditation practice.

We are living righteously when our thoughts, feelings, and
actions are honest, appropriate, and entirely constructive and
life-enhancing. Behaviors which are dishonest, inappropriate, or
harmful to ourselves, others, or the planet should always be
avoided. Right living nurtures psychological and physical health
and attunes us to nature's cosmic forces which can then be supportive of us.

See the Wholeness of Life and Fulfill These
Four Primary Aspirations of the Heart

The primary aspirations of the heart (our true Self) are:

1. *The inherent inclination of nature to uphold and maintain the
cosmic order.* When we are always in harmony with it because
of wise and appropriate use of our abilities and knowledge, it
supports and provides for us. Our lives should be unrestricted.
The "work" that we do and the actions we perform should be
enjoyable and almost effortless.
2. *Satisfaction of wholesome desires.* They can most easily be
satisfied by eliminating unwholesome and nonuseful cravings

and implementing causes that will produce desired results. Causative actions can be creative visualization, gentle intention, expectation, and physical actions as necessary. The use of imagination, intention, and expectation are creative actions performed in awareness and in the mind that elicit a response from omnipresent Consciousness and Cosmic Mind.

3. *Affluence—to be in a continuous flow of resources, events, circumstances, and relationships for our highest good.* We are then truly prosperous because the spiritual, mental, emotional, physical, and environmental components of our lives are harmoniously integrated. Conscious or subconscious resistance to the flow of supportive events not only limits our ability to enjoy good fortune in the mundane realm, it is an obstacle to spiritual growth.

4. *Liberation of consciousness, the ultimate aim of every incarnated soul.* Do not make the mistake of thinking that you can or will effect psychological transformation and concentrate on spiritual growth after you have accomplished the first three aims. Nurture psychological transformation and spiritual growth while you are finding your right place in the cosmic order, fulfilling wholesome desires, and learning to be in the flow of good fortune. Avoid thinking that if you give most of your attention to cloistered spiritual practices while ignoring your mundane duties and the need to be effectively functional that "everything will work out one way or another."

Master Your Attention

For where your treasure is, there will be your heart also.

                                                  – The Gospel of Matthew 6:21

Powers of concentration can be developed. Preoccupation with self-centered concerns, apathy, purposelessness, mental confusion, emotional unrest, sleep deprivation, and tiredness may contribute to inability to be attentive. Interest in what is perceived, zest for life, purposefulness, rationality, emotional stability, and high energy levels are characteristics of individuals whose powers of concentration are well-developed. Meditation practice also improves powers of concentration.

Focus your attention on important matters; disregard what is not important. Mastery of attention in the midst of activities will enable you to meditate more effectively and attentive practice of meditation will enable you to live more effectively. Don't say that you cannot concentrate; train yourself to do it. Avoid daydreaming, erratic mental conversations, idle talk (and gossip) with others, and excessive association with others who are always confused and disorganized. Have meaningful purposes. Plan your actions and stay on course. Find out what you can do to succeed, and do it.

Think Rationally

Our destiny, our being's heart and home, is with infinitude, and only there. – *William Wordsworth (1770 – 1850)*

Rational thinking is orderly and reasonable (realistic). The mind of a person who is irrational is confused, facts are mixed with erroneous ideas and illusions, and discernment is lacking. Of such a person, we may say, "He doesn't have any common sense." Avoid allowing emotions to dominate reason. Some people allow their emotions to dominate their thinking and behavior. They say, "I feel that I should do this." If by "feeling" we are attempting to describe an intuitive awareness of what should be done, we can go forward. Cultivate your powers of discriminative intelligence and discern the difference between compulsive urges or whims and intuitive insight.

Be Emotionally Stable

That one who has faith acquires God-knowledge. Devoted to that, controlling the senses, and having wisdom, the devotee quickly attains the tranquil state. – *The Bhagavad Gita 4:39*

Be emotionally stable by cultivating Self-contentment at all times. Remember, your real Self is your spiritual essence. Be anchored in that. Experience appropriate feelings without allowing them to overwhelm your powers of reason. If feelings related to past events arise and cause discomfort, be objective as you confront the situation in your mind and resolve it. As a spiritual being you are superior to your mind and its contents. Choose to be emotionally calm and stable. Be inwardly strong and Self-responsible for your feelings, thoughts, and actions.

Nurture Supportive Relationships

To be truly united in knowledge, love, and service with all beings, and thus to realize one's self in the all-pervading God is the essence of goodness. – *Rabindranath Tagore (1861 – 1941)*

To have supportive human relationships, be supportive of others without becoming overly involved in petty situations or immature, dependent relationships.

To have the support of nature, cooperate with its laws by thinking constructively, living wisely, eating intelligently, and obtaining sufficient sleep. Exercise regularly in ways which are ideal for your basic mind-body constitution.

To have the support of Cosmic Mind, always be optimistic and think rationally. Remember that your mental states and habitual thoughts constantly interact with Cosmic Mind which is responsive to them. Optimistic people who are aware of having a relationship with God usually live longer and are healthier than people who are pessimistic and feel alienated.

To have the support of God's grace, learn to be receptive to it. Do your best to help yourself accomplish your purposes while having faith in the "goodness" of life. When unplanned good fortune is experienced, be thankful.

Use Time, Energy, Resources, and
and Skills Wisely and Productively

Spiritual growth can be quickened by condensing experiences with concentrated endeavor. – *Paramahansa Yogananda (1893 – 1952)*

When attention and actions are focused on matters which are important and unimportant matters are ignored or only given minimal attention, goals are achieved and purposes are fulfilled more rapidly.

* You cannot control time; choose what you will do in the time that is available to you. Do the important things first. Improve your efficiency to accomplish everything you want to accomplish.
* Don't waste vital energies with idle talk, worry, irregular lifestyle routines, or poor health habits. Conserved energies can be transmuted to strengthen the mind and the immune system.
* Use money and other material resources constructively.
* Be skillfully effective and success-oriented.

People who are dysfunctional, or have the potential to live effectively but do little to improve their circumstances, do not experience success on the spiritual path. They are inclined to be small-minded and complacent, behave erratically, and desire lifestyle circumstances and personal relationships that will provide feelings of emotional security.

There is no permanent value in clinging to ordinary states of consciousness. Be intent on discovering the truth about you, God, and your relationship with the Infinite. Do all that you can to quicken your spiritual growth. Lack of knowledge is not a major obstacle because knowledge can be acquired. Purposelessness and laziness are the two self-limiting characteristics that need to be renounced.

Banish Troubled Thoughts and Feelings

He to whom all things are one and who draws all things to one and sees all things in one may be stable in heart and peaceably abide in God. *– Thomas À Kempis (1380 – 1471)*

Fear, anxiety, worry, or confusion cannot prevail in a mind that is illumined by Self-knowledge. Dramatizing (or being preoccupied or obsessed with) troubled thoughts and feelings is a debilitating habit that weakens will power, depresses the body's immune system, stresses the nervous system, clouds intelligence, nurtures moods of despair, and interferes with endeavors to live effectively. When necessary, replace troubled thoughts and feelings with positive thoughts and feelings of well-being.

When mentally or emotionally unsettled, do something to engage your attention. Go for a brisk walk, exercise until you feel pleasantly exhilarated, or do something else that attracts and focuses your attention and restores orderly thinking. Be more purposeful. Expand your awareness. Be Self-confident. Let feelings of zest for life rise up from within you. Cultivate cheerfulness and soul-contentment.

Be Totally Committed to Your Spiritual Path

God is Infinite; and to love the boundless, reaching on from grace to grace, adding charity to faith, and rising upwards ever to see the ideal— that is to love God. – Frederick William Robertson (1816 – 1853)

When you know your spiritual path, be totally committed to it. Read metaphysical literature written by someone who was (or is) enlightened. Improve your intellectual powers so that you will be able to discern what is true. Be faithful to your spiritual tradition while respecting the rights of others to follow their path. Don't mix (adulterate and make impure) your valid philosophical knowledge with theories and opinions expressed by others who are not yet Self-realized.

Adhere to a meditation routine until you can experience superconsciousness at will, then go more deeply to experience refined, transcendent superconscious states. By patient practice, learn to be superconscious after meditation. When ordinary awareness and superconsciousness coexist, superior superconscious influences weaken and neutralize harmful subconscious influences, purify the mind, refine the nervous system, and elicit cosmic conscious states. These spontaneous processes are known by devotees who are totally committed to psychological transformation and Self-realization. They are not known by truth students whose primary desire is to experience pleasant moods, have fleeting "revelations," or acquire enough understanding to allow them to live a more comfortable life.

It is not necessary to talk with others about philosophical concepts or spiritual practices. Acquire necessary knowledge and diligently apply it to verify it by your own experience. If you know someone who is spiritually awake, be inspired by their example while attending to your own spiritual growth.

Surrender any remaining sense of illusional selfhood. This is most easily done by acknowledging your changeless essence of being. At first, you may have a weak or unclear intellectual grasp of what you are. As you continue to contemplate the matter, you may have sudden, fleeting insights. Eventually, you will experience a shift of viewpoint that enables a clear apprehension of your real nature.

How long will it take to be Self-realized? It will require as much time as needed. Self-realization can occur quickly or it may emerge progressively. Because it is your destiny to be Self-realized, you have no other choice that is of comparable value.

Meditate in the Om Vibration

In the beginning was the Word [Greek, *Logos*], and the Word was [is] with God, and the Word was [is] God. – *Gospel of John 1:1*

The evidential aspect of God is Om. Meditation on Om culminates in knowledge of its meaning and in Self- and God-realization.
– *Patanjali's yoga-sutras 1:27,28*

The vibration of the power of Consciousness emanating from the Godhead or Oversoul aspect of supreme Consciousness is described as the Word or Om (Aum). Because it is the primary self-expression of Consciousness it is the most obvious and accessible aspect of God on which to concentrate and with which to identify when aspiring to transcendental realizations.

You can meditate *in* Om like this:

- Sit in your preferred meditation posture. If you have a routine of practice for calming the mind, start with that. When your mind is calm, proceed to the next stage.
- Direct your attention to the space between the eyebrows. Also be aware in the higher brain. Look into the spiritual eye while listening in both ears. If you see light, observe it and blend your awareness with it. If you do not see light, do not strain to see it; just gaze into inner space. If you hear subtle inner sounds, listen to them. Gently endeavor to hear a subtler sound behind the sound (or sounds) that you first hear. Continue until the sound that you hear is constant. Merge your awareness in it. Contemplate that which is beyond light and sound: the unbounded field of infinite Consciousness. Learn to enjoy the deep silence.
- Conclude your practice session when you want to do so.

When first practicing this meditation technique, you may cover your eyes with your hands and close the ear openings by pressing gently with your thumbs against the small protrusions in front of the ear opening. With external light and sound excluded, you may be better able to inwardly concentrate. The placement of the hands will make concentration more intentional. After a while, you can return your hands to your lap and continue to look and listen within. Melt in the sound and omnipresence.

When you pray for yourself, or others, or when you want to accomplish a purpose, heal a condition, or have your circumstances improved, first meditate in Om, then do your inner work in that awareness of wholeness in God. Do this with alert attention and clear intention. When you are firmly established in awareness of the Om vibration, even a gentle intention to have a desire fulfilled or a need met will compel Cosmic Mind and cosmic forces to respond in ways which are most appropriate.

Affirmation
Knowing my true relationship with the Infinite,
I always live wisely with conscious intention.

TWELVE

Our Freedom of Choice and God's Grace

Among truth seekers who want to live effectively and have an intimate relationship with the Infinite, two subjects of interest are 1) freedom of personal choice and 2) God's grace.

How much freedom do we really have? How can we know what to choose? What is grace and what role does it play in our lives? Can we obstruct the flows of grace by being too insistent on using our free will? To explore these matters we need to have a basic understanding of our true nature, God, and the universe in which we presently live. It is necessary to look beyond concepts we might have in regard to God as being a cosmic person with humanlike characteristics or egocentric inclinations.

God and Cosmic (Universal) Mind

Enlivening impulses in the field of infinite Consciousness which support and nurture orderly unfoldments that occur in the universe are referred to as the actions of grace.

- *The universal, impersonal laws of cause and effect.* Every event that occurs has a corresponding cause. A physical force causes an effect equal to the force that is exerted; our physical actions produce effects which correspond to them. What is not generally known is that thoughts, imagination, and will can also produce effects. The laws of cause and effect are universal: applicable everywhere. Being impersonal, they are influential regardless of who or what originates a cause.
- *The metaphysical (beyond the physical) law of attraction.* We can attract events and circumstances by thinking about them and by imagining that we already have them. When we do this, we discover that there is no separation between mind

and matter. We may attract events and circumstances and not be aware of having done so. By conscious control of thinking and states of awareness, we can attract supportive events and improve the quality of our lives.

• *The mixed results of acquiescence (passive consent).* Some of the circumstances (and relationships) we have, whether agreeable or disagreeable, may not be the results of our intentional planning. We may have allowed ourselves to be attracted to them because of our curiosity, boredom, loneliness, apathy, lack of courage to refuse, or lack of a clear sense of purpose.

Some unplanned events are fortunate; others may be troublesome or cause discomfort or pain. When allowing ourselves to be drawn into circumstances chosen by others, we should be discerning, to know whether the situation will be 1) worthwhile; 2) useless or debilitating; 3) a distraction that turns us from our major purposes; 4) evidence of grace.

Most of the experiences and circumstances we will have in the near and distant future will be determined by our choices and by God's grace.

• To choose is to select from possible alternatives, to decide in accord with preference. It is better to make important choices when the mind is calm and thinking is rational. If we are impulsive or mentally confused, if emotions dominate reason, or we are too easily influenced by the opinions of others, our choices may not be wise. Choices made on the basis of subconscious conditioning, or habit, are usually not for our highest good. When possible, avoid making important choices when tired, stressed, deprived of sleep, others are demanding a decision, or late at night (when it is easy to have conscious thoughts mixed with and influenced by inclinations from the subconscious level of the mind).

• Streams of grace are always flowing and can be influential in our lives when we are receptive to it. We often experience the benefits of grace even when we are not expecting them or not consciously able to make ourselves receptive to them. Because the actions of grace are impersonal, their influences are immediately evident when and where they can be expressive.

The choices we made in the past and our actions and reactions to events made impressions in the mind which remain as memories. Many memories are neutral; they do not influence us. Other memories may either have constructive influences or cause discomfort. It is usually all right to allow constructive subconscious inclinations to be expressive. If they are inclined to reinforce addictive or self-defeating behaviors, they can be resisted, weakened, and neutralized by will power, positive thinking, the cultivation of clear states of awareness, regular superconscious meditation practice, and intentional living. Eventually, all destructive subconscious drives will be replaced by entirely constructive inclinations. When superconsciousness is permanent, all of our thoughts, feelings, and actions will be appropriate for every occasion because soul-impelled.

Many of the problems and troublesome situations people have are not karmic (caused by past thoughts or actions). They are the results of self-centered, negative thinking which is intentionally nurtured or allowed to prevail, a confused state of awareness, or unwise behaviors—all of which can easily be improved by decisive choices and constructive actions.

Suffering which has not yet been experienced is to be avoided.
    – *Patanjali's yoga sutras 2:16*

The Liberating Effects of Assuming
Ideal Mental States and States of Awareness

Is virtue a thing remote? I wish to be virtuous, and lo!, virtue is at hand. – *Attributed to Confucius (551 – 479 B.C.E.)*

To allow destructive subconscious inclinations to prevail is to play the role of a victim. Remember your true nature in relationship to the Infinite. *Assume* that view, and think, feel, and act in accord with it. Exercise freedom of choice and liberate yourself

How to Remove, and Rise Above, Harmful Subconscious Influences

1. View subconscious inclinations and thoughts or feelings related to memories without emotional response. You will then be able to think rationally, make wise choices, and live effectively.

2. When remembering an unpleasant experience, if you feel overwhelmed by confused thoughts and strong emotions:
   a. Remember that memories have no power to influence you without your consent. Cultivate soul peace.
   b. If disordered thoughts and/or strong emotions cannot be immediately controlled, *take a few deep breaths* to restore your sense of self-command and to discharge and release emotions related to memories.

3. Weaken and eliminate harmful subconscious influences by resisting them and implementing constructive thoughts, feelings, and actions.

4. Use your powers of discriminative intelligence to discern the difference between your true, pure-conscious nature and the contents of your mind.

5. Cultivate superconscious states until you are permanently established in Self-knowledge.

from the bondage of conditions you do not want in your life.

When you become aware of false beliefs that prevent you from thinking rationally, renounce them. Likewise, banish all illusions by choosing to accurately perceive what you observe.

Scan your memories without having emotional reactions to them; they are only impressions of past perceptions stored in the subconscious level of your mind. Emotional reactions to memories make new impressions in the mind. When you can dispassionately view memories of unpleasant events (failure, rejection, loss, mistakes, painful incidents of any kind) they are powerless to influence you.

When circumstances require you to perform skillfully, or when starting a worthwhile project, assume a mental attitude and state of awareness which will enable you to proceed with confidence. Cooperate with the universal laws of cause and effect to have the full support of nature's forces. Use the law of attraction to accomplish purposes which are of value.

How to Be Responsive to the Impulses of the Creative Intelligence That Pervades the Universe

The intelligence of infinite Consciousness is creative; its impulses produce results. Its influence is evident everywhere, from the pure realm of existence-being to the physical universe.

It is normal to desire what is needed for comfort and well-being. We should not have to struggle or use most of our time and energy to acquire necessary things and have ideal circumstances. Preoccupation with material aims confines awareness and inclines us to ignore or neglect the importance of life's ultimate purpose. When we understand life's processes and know how to live effectively, we can more easily provide for ourselves and be receptive to the good fortune that can and will be provided by God's grace.

What about people who are religious, who sincerely love God and pray for God's help, yet are impoverished? Religious beliefs and practices, however sincere, do not improve one's personal

Use Your Creative Imagination

Creative imagination enables you to mentally picture and attract or produce what does not yet exist. Vividly imagine what you want to have or experience and know that the laws of cause and effect can actualize it for you.

You are already using your imagination; now use it in a controlled, creative manner. Instead of merely wishing for ideal circumstances, imagine them as they can be. If you cannot imagine ideal circumstances, imagine (and feel at the deepest level of your being) that circumstances that are for your highest good already exist.

If you can do something to assist the actualization process, do it. If you do not know what to do, or cannot do anything, be optimistic. Maintain your faith that Cosmic Mind and God's grace can and will unfold results that are ideal for you (and for others if you want to assist them).

Use creative imagination to be physically, mentally, and emotionally healthy; to satisfy wholesome desires; and to harmonize all aspects of your life. Use it to live effectively and to quicken your spiritual growth. See yourself as being skillfully functional and steadily progressing through the stages of spiritual growth. See yourself as an intelligent, disciplined, purposeful, ethical, successful, prosperous, and happy person. See all of the ideal circumstances you are worthy of having, and claim them for yourself.

Never use creative imagination in an endeavor to control or manipulate others. Desire that they may be as free as you desire to be.

circumstances if the mind is not somewhat illumined, and behaviors are not conformed to higher levels of understanding. Belief in God does not always make an obvious difference in our everyday lives, although it may confer a degree of mental and emotional peace. God-realization illumines the mind and enables us to know our relationship with the wholeness of Consciousness, the realm of limitless possibilities.

The experiences and circumstances of individuals who will not, or cannot, awaken to higher levels of spiritual awareness will continue to correspond to their habitual mental states, states of consciousness, and behaviors. Their conditions will improve when their awareness is clarified and more effective functional skills are acquired and used. Spiritually unaware people who are only partially conscious struggle because of their delusions and illusions and are impelled by habits and the urgings of their subconscious conditionings. They may not know that what they consider to be their "life" is but a fleeting episode in a much longer sojourn in space-time.

It may not seem fair that so many people in our world of abundance and opportunity experience limitation. The laws of cause and effect are unyielding. When we live in accord with them, we prosper and grow spiritually; when we do otherwise, we create or attract misfortune.

If we do not yet know how to live effectively, we can learn. If we are suffering, we can discover its cause and eliminate it. If we are unhappy, we can choose to be happy. If we feel lonely and removed from God, we can be fulfilled by discovering our innate wholeness and relationship with the Infinite.

Be a spiritual scientist. Experiment with these processes to have your own experiences in regard to their usefulness. As you progress, your knowledge will blossom into wisdom.

Fulfill Your Spiritual Destiny

When you are partially Self-realized, God-realization will not be complete. When you are fully Self-realized, you will also be fully God-realized. Thus Self- and God-realized, with your mind purified and illumined, you will be liberated.

Some truth seekers desire only to have enough Self- and God-knowledge to allow them to live a more comfortable human existence. Some desire to acquire exceptional abilities in order to have more control over others or their circumstances. Wise devotees of God know that only complete illumination of consciousness is liberating.

Affirmation
Established in Self- and God-awareness, I make wise choices, think and act constructively, live decisively, and am always receptive to the impulses of grace.

People often think that for our will to find rest in God's means a fatalistic resignation to the will of God. But frequently the passive will of such people finds this impossible, because their active will has not found its way into God's will. How can they find the way by night if they haven't looked for it by day?

– Albert Schweitzer (1875 – 1965)
Reverence for Life

THIRTEEN

How to Have Peace of Mind in a Changing World

At the innermost level of our being, we are serene. Only the surface level of our awareness can be disturbed.

Cosmic Forces That Can Influence the Mind and Consciousness

The existence of subtle, cosmic forces that can influence mental states and states of awareness are known by only a few people who have the intellectual capacity to comprehend them. Paramahansa Yogananda's guru, Swami Sri Yukteswar, explained his views regarding the influences of cosmic forces in a small book, *The Holy Science*, first published in India in 1894. The following, brief overview provides insight into this timely subject:

Centuries ago, sages in India taught a theory of time-cycles to explain the influences of cosmic forces on human beings and evolutionary trends on our planet. Their calculations were based on the idea that forces from the center of our galaxy influence the electromagnetic field of the solar system and the mental and intellectual faculties of its human inhabitants.

When our solar system is at the most distant point from the galactic center, human powers of perception and intellect are weak, soul awareness is obscured, and ignorance of the facts of life prevails. When our sun and its planets are nearest to the galactic center, powers of perception are refined, intellectual abilities are pronounced, soul awareness is more evident, and spiritual enlightenment is more common.

The duration of one complete time-cycle is 24,000 solar years.

Sub-cycles (eras) within this grand cycle are designated as a 1,200-year ascending era of confusion during which most people are able to comprehend only what can be perceived by the senses; a 2,400-year era during which comprehension and utilization of electric, magnetic, and atomic forces is possible; a 3,600-year era during which mental and intellectual powers are highly developed; a 4,800-year era during which intuitive powers are unveiled and many people are spiritually enlightened. This era is followed by another 4,800-year era during which the mental and intellectual faculties of most people will begin to diminish as the sun and solar system begin to move away from the galactic enter.

We are now in the early phase of an ascending 2,400-year era as indicated by the rapid advancement of science and technology during the past two hundred years. During transition phases from one era to another, influences of both eras are blended for a few hundred years. Although we are currently discovering and utilizing subtle forces in nature, beginning to develop mental and intellectual powers, and learning to apprehend and appreciate the existence of higher realities, influences of the recent era of confusion are still obvious in the collective consciousness of people. Half of the estimated six billion people on earth are impoverished; one-third are illiterate; regional wars are common; racial, cultural, and religious intolerance exists; extreme political and fundamentalist religious opinions are promoted; crimes are committed; and millions of people of all age groups lack a clear sense of meaningful purpose for their lives.

On a more positive note: more people are healthier and living longer and productively, are better educated, and are interested in learning how to elicit and actualize their innate, divine qualities. The current trend of evolution is supportive of all who are willing to learn how to cooperate with it. During the 21st century, conditions will become more harmonious, poverty and illiteracy will be greatly reduced, and hundreds of millions of people will be sincerely engaged in cultivating spirituality to benefit themselves and society.

Regardless of the era in which we live, when aspiration to Self- and God realization is compelling, rapid spiritual growth is possible. When we are spiritually aware, we are impervious to environmental influence of all kinds. Thus, even in an era of confusion, we can be enlightened. Since the events and circumstances we encounter correspond to our mental states, states of awareness, and behaviors, our experiences will be fortunate.

Choose to Live Freely, Effectively, and Enjoyably

Until we are spiritually enlightened, our lives may be adversely influenced by our negative thoughts, uncontrolled moods, subconscious conditionings, unwise or inappropriate behaviors or actions, or the opinions and behaviors of others.

To live freely, effectively, and enjoyably:

- Think constructively. Refuse to allow negative thoughts to distort your mind and awareness. Nourish your mind with your own positive thoughts and the positive ideas of others. Read inspirational literature.
- Emotions are a feeling-response to our urges or thoughts or to events we observe or hear about. They can be controlled by cultivating soul-awareness and Self-reliance. Allow only emotions which enhance your life to prevail.
- Refuse to allow negative subconscious inclinations or tendencies to influence your mental states, emotions, actions, or reactions. Replace negative inclinations and habits with positive thoughts, feelings, and actions. In time, negative subconscious conditionings will be weakened and their forces will be constructively transmuted. When the soul force that was formerly confined by negative subconscious states is released, it will empower your life.
- Perform all actions with rational, decisive intention.
- Disregard the faulty opinions and misguided behaviors of others. Cultivate your powers of intellectual and intuitive discernment and live in the highest and best way without being unduly influenced by what others say or do.

Be receptive to and thankful for the good fortune that you create or attract or that is provided for you. Don't feel guilty if you have good fortune and others do not; they, too, can learn to live freely, effectively, and enjoyably if they desire to do so.

• Create ideal circumstances by using your powers of rational thinking and imagination and the skills that you have. If more knowledge is needed, acquire it. If your functional abilities need to be improved, improve them. You are in this world to learn, grow, and excel; do it.

• Attract resources and supportive events and circumstances by cultivating an optimistic mental attitude that will make you receptive to them. Renounce thoughts of limitation and self-destructive behaviors. Choose to be prosperous in all aspects of your life: thrive, flourish, and be successful.

• Accept the supportive resources, events, and circumstances that are provided for you by nature, God's grace, and the beneficial actions of others. Because we abide in God's wholeness, much of what we need for our well-being is already freely provided; we only have to learn to perceive and accept it. However your good fortune is made possible, be thankful for it.

Effectively Relate to External Conditions

Events and circumstances are always changing; observe them with dispassionate objectivity while remaining inwardly calm and discerning. You will then live peacefully without being overly influenced by external conditions. Truth students who know they are spiritual beings and who know the reality of God and the natural laws that cause effects to occur, have peace of mind in the midst of changing circumstances.

Your temporary sojourn in space-time provides you with many opportunities to learn, unfold innate knowledge, improve your abilities, and grow to emotional and spiritual maturity. Use your available time and your skills to become aware of and actualize your full potential.

You are not a mortal, physical creature aspiring, hoping, or trying to become a spiritual being—you are an immortal unit of God's being relating to the human condition. Think and live in accord with your highest understanding. If your thinking is unclear, exercise your power of choice to think decisively. If your actions are erratic, be more purposeful. Be the master of your mental and emotional states and behaviors.

Faithfully adhere to your wholesome lifestyle routines and spiritual practices and you will always be cheerful, optimistic, energetic, and enthusiastic. It will then be easy to direct your attention to matters of importance and to ignore those which are of little or no value.

Every day, calm the waves of the mind by meditating until you are established in superconsciousness. After meditation, train yourself to be superconscious when you are engaged in normal activities and relationships. You will then be able to relate to this world while also aware of a larger Reality.

Nurture Self- and God-awareness. Think and act rationally and contemplate your relationship with the Infinite. Expand your awareness. Cultivate a cosmic conscious outlook.

The clarity of your awareness will unfailingly ensure your well-being and your exemplary life will bless others.

Affirmation
Ever established in Self- and God-awareness,
I am poised and peaceful.

Direct love toward God, and peace comes over the soul: turn it from God, and the heart becomes a broken fountain where tears fall "from the sighful branches of [the] mind." – *Fulton J. Sheen (1895 – 1979)*

FOURTEEN

The Life-Enhancing Effects
Of Positive Affirmation

An *invisible source* provides events and resources for our well-being and good fortune. Whatever exists in the mundane realm emerges from that inexhaustible source. When we are always established in conscious awareness of the reality of God's presence, we know that our highest good is assured.

How to Use Affirmations

The purpose of using affirmations is not to condition the mind; it is to awaken to a state of awareness which will allow you to see and experience ideal events and circumstances.

By affirmative thinking and speaking you can experience a positive change in how you view yourself and your relationship to God and the world. As your mind is refreshed and your spiritual awareness increases, your life will be transformed and appropriate circumstances will harmoniously unfold.

Forceful, emotional affirmation is neither necessary nor recommended. Calm, alert, absorption of attention and awareness in the process is the best way to ensure satisfying results. Rather that to allow whims, compulsions, or a sense of desperate need to express as immature, willfulness, be wisdom-guided.

Gently use will power or almost effortless intention to concentrate. Because you are a spiritual being, all that is included in God's wholeness is available to you now to the extent that you can perceive, acknowledge, and accept it.

When composing an affirmation, first clearly define your specific purpose and write it with conscious intention. Know the meaning of the words you use.

Example #1:

My clear, unwavering, soul-inspired perception of real possibilities strengthens my resolve, energizes my mind, empowers my purposeful actions, and enables me to be immediately responsive to the enlivening, supportive impulses of God's providential grace.

- **my** Indicates possession.
- **clear** Devoid of flaws or blemishes.
- **unwavering** Steady, resolute, determined.
- **soul-inspired** An urge or inclination to create or to do something that is meaningful impelled from the innermost core of your being. Thus inspired, it is easier to imagine—to mentally "see" and feel to be real—the highest good that is possible for yourself and others.
- **perception** Seeing, observing, being aware.
- **real possibilities** What is real exists. What is possible can occur. Real possibilities that exist in your mind and consciousness can definitely be acknowledged and actualized.
- **strengthens** Makes stronger.
- **resolve** A firm decision to accomplish a purpose.
- **energizes** Imparts energy.
- **mind** The faculty of thinking, reasoning, and imagining.
- **empowers** Invests with authority and supports freedom of choice and action.
- **purposeful actions** Intentional, goal-directed actions that make possible the fulfillment of desires.
- **enables** Provides the means, knowledge, and opportunity to do something.
- **immediately** Directly, without delay.
- **responsive** Prompt acknowledgment.
- **enlivening** Animating, imbuing with spiritual influence.
- **supportive** That which upholds or maintains.
- **impulses** Compelling forces.
- **God** The one Being, Life, and Power.
- **providential** Provided by divine influences.
- **grace** Care, provision freely bestowed.

Example #2:

My constant, conscious awareness of the presence of God
assures the continuous, appropriate, and timely unfoldments
of supportive events and circumstances for my highest good.

- **constant** Firm, steadfast, unchanging.
- **conscious** Awake, alert.
- **awareness** Perception.
- **presence** Something existing here and now.
- **assures** Makes certain.
- **continuous** Uninterrupted, unbroken.
- **appropriate** Most suitable, ideal, or right for the situation or occasion.
- **timely** Occurring at an opportune time.
- **unfoldments** Emerging circumstances.
- **supportive** That which upholds or maintains.
- **events** What happens, outcomes.
- **circumstances** Conditions, modes, or states.
- **highest good** Circumstances which are most supportive of our total well-being.

Affirmations are not to be thought of or used as magical incantations composed and recited to cause specific effects or to manipulate or control other people. Avoid trying to impress your subconscious mind with the concept defined by your affirmative theme. Disregard all thoughts, ideas, and feelings which are incompatible with your inner vision of possibilities.

- Read the affirmation to comprehend its meaning.
- Quietly speak it aloud two or three times with concentrated intention and resolute conviction.
- Speak it mentally two or three times, with certainty, while expanding your awareness to vividly apprehend that which you want to perceive and experience.
- See, with inner vision, your highest good in all aspects of your life. *Feel* it at the soul level. Be thankful.

- Keep the outcome of the affirmation established in your awareness as you attend to your duties and perform any necessary purposeful activities. If you cannot do anything to assist the actualization of your heart's desire, maintain your faith in the supportive actions of the universe and the impulses of God's grace within and around you.

A 31-Day Affirmative Spiritual Practice Program

Acknowledge your true nature as a spiritual being. As you speak affirmative words, feel and intuitively apprehend the presence of God within and around you. Let your thoughts, decisions, and actions always be determined by your highest understanding and soul inclinations.

An ideal time to use affirmations is after an interlude of quiet meditation. They can also be used at other times.

Each morning, read an affirmation. Speak it aloud two or three times. Mentally affirm it two or three times. Assume the mental attitude, feeling, and state of consciousness that you affirm. During the day, keep the theme in your awareness and conform your thinking, feeling, and actions to it.

1. I acknowledge that I am a spiritual being.

2. I am always fully aware of the wholeness of God within and around me.

3. I am always peaceful, happy, attentive, and respectful of others as I efficiently perform my necessary and chosen duties.

4. I perceive the realm of nature as a manifestation of the cosmic forces emanated from God's being.

5. I remain established in soul contentment in all circumstances.

6. I nourish my mind with only constructive thoughts.

7. I am always cheerful and optimistic.

8. My intellectual powers are keen and discerning.

9. My thinking is rational and I make wise decisions.

10. I am always in my right place in the universe.

11. My life-enhancing desires are always easily fulfilled.

12. I am always in the flow of good fortune.

13. The universe always spontaneously and appropriately provides for all of my needs.

14. I see the needs of others and do what I can to help them.

15. I see the hurts of others and do what I can to heal them.

16. I am good to the planet and it is good to me.

17. When I pray, I pray *in* God.

18. As I meditate *in* God I awaken to conscious awareness of my real Self.

19. I am regularly attentive to my daily self-care routines for my overall health and well-being.

20. I enjoy my daily interlude of solitude.

21. Ever established in clear awareness of the presence of God, I live happily with confidence and enthusiasm.

22. I balance productive activities with regular occasions of rest and recreational activities.

23. I know myself to be an agent through which God's power flows and creatively expresses.

24. I live effectively with conscious intention.

25. I always have a clear sense of meaningful purpose.

26. I wisely perform creative actions without mental or emotional attachment to them or to their constructive results.

27. In and behind the face of nature I perceive the reality of God.

28. With my intelligence and intuition I easily discern truth from untruth.

29. I am totally committed to God-conscious living.

30. As I become increasingly cosmic conscious I perceive myself and everything as existing in the one, infinite Consciousness.

31. Renouncing all delusions and illusions, I live skillfully and effectively with flawless understanding.

Write An Affirmation For Yourself

Sit quietly. Be still and silent until you are soul-centered and God-aware. Think about your life, your relationship with the Infinite, your personal circumstances, and the possibilities that are before you.

In your private journal or on a sheet of paper, clearly and decisively write an affirmation that accurately defines what you want to experience or accomplish. Write it as though the desired outcome is already a fact.

Speak the words aloud a few times with confidence.

Speak them in your mind a few times.

Take the affirmative ideal into the deepest level of your being and realize it superconsciously.

Let your beneficial change in outlook and your decisive actions, when necessary, produce the results.

Affirmation
I speak only words of truth and see them manifest.

The finite mind generates countless ideas which weaken it and veil perception of truth. These cause impressions and tendencies in the mind which are, for the most part, latent or dormant. When the mind is rid of them, the veil vanishes in a moment like mist at sunrise, and with it the greatest of sorrows also vanish. – *Ancient Yoga Text*

FIFTEEN

What You Will Know and Do
When You are Enlightened

Because you are a unit of the infinite field of Consciousness, you will exist forever. Knowing this, ask: How am I living my immortal life?

What are your thoughts and feelings as you ponder this question? Write them on a sheet of paper or in your personal journal and refer to them from time to time.

Are you satisfied that you are on the right course in life, or do you need to make some constructive changes? If you are certain that you are on the right course, adhere to it. If you need to make constructive changes, do so.

If you have thoughts or feelings of regret or sadness about your past behaviors or present circumstances, examine them, come to terms with them, then discard them.

At the core of your being, you are serene, knowledgeable, and competent. Nurture your divine qualities and actualize them. Look forward to the many possibilities that you have to learn, grow, and serve.

- You will rise above ordinary states of awareness to superconscious and cosmic conscious states.
- You will know that you are not a physical creature hoping, trying, or vainly struggling to improve your conditions and circumstances or become more spiritually aware.
- Clarification and expansion of your awareness will enable you to more easily discern your real Self in relationship to the wholeness of life.
- You will be truly happy.

- Your awakened spiritual forces will vitalize your body.
- Your mind will be illumined.
- Your intellectual and intuitive powers will improve.
- Your extraordinary powers of perception and exceptional abilities will enable you to live skillfully and effectively.
- Resources for your total well-being and to enable you to accomplish your meaningful purposes will be provided.
- Circumstances and relationships for your highest good will unfold harmoniously.
- Supportive events will spontaneously occur.
- Your appreciation for life and living will be enhanced.
- You will rapidly awaken through the remaining stages of spiritual growth.
- Erroneous ideas will be replaced by flawless knowledge of what is true.
- Accurate perceptions will replace illusions.
- You will live freely without limitations of any kind.
- You will realize that you have ever been, are, and will ever be an immortal spiritual being.
- Your thoughts and actions will be effortlessly conformed to the rhythms of cosmic processes which will fully support you in all of your wisdom-directed endeavors.
- Knowledge of the reality of God and the processes of life will be revealed from within you.
- Your fully unfolded Self- and God-realization will silently bless others and spiritually enliven them.
- The collective consciousness of everyone on Planet Earth will be elevated by your enlightened consciousness.
- Your inner light will shine.

Regardless of whether you are new on the spiritual path or have been avidly studying and practicing for many years, be assured that with unwavering aspiration and right endeavor your progress will be satisfying and the desire of your heart to be fully awake will be gloriously fulfilled. The invisible, yet tangible reality of God will be increasingly supportive of you as you become more attuned to its constant presence and learn to be responsive to its will—its inherent inclination to fulfill its purposes through and as you.

Having decided to accomplish the ultimate purpose of your life, be firmly committed to it. Don't look back, or allow your attention to be distracted. Diligently attend to your duties and spiritual practices. Concentrate on what is yet to be realized with complete confidence in your abilities and in God's grace.

There has never been a better time than now to engage in intensive analysis of the nature of Consciousness and spiritual practice. Conform your thoughts and actions with the trends of evolution and let the power of God have its way with your life. Do your part to help yourself. Grace will do the rest.

Speak These Words With Conviction
I know I am an immortal spiritual being with
all knowledge of infinite Consciousness and the
processes of life within me. Established in this
understanding, I think rationally, act wisely,
and live skillfully and effectively.

Like a drop of water from the sea and a grain of sand, so are a few years in the day of eternity.
      – The Old Testament Apocrypha (Ecclesiasticus 18:10)

Answers to Questions

Answers to Questions

Can God-realization be accomplished in one incarnation? I did not become interested in spiritual matters until after my fiftieth birthday. I am in good health. Is there enough time left for me to become God-realized before I depart from this world?

Yes. Your present incarnation is the only one that is real to you. If you will allow your innate urge to be fully awake to inspire your thoughts and actions, your spiritual growth—awakening to the truth of what you are—can be rapid.

A sincere desire to be spiritually awake is more important than the number of years you have been on this planet. You probably have several decades ahead of you; use your available time wisely.

I have only recently started to seek the truth about myself and the meaning of life. Many of the ideas and philosophical concepts I encounter are new to me. Some are contrary to what I have believed or have been taught. How should I proceed?

Be curious and open-minded, but not gullible. Use your powers of intellectual discernment to determine what is true and disregard what is not true. To the extent that it is possible to do so, test what you learn to verify it. Be guided by your intelligence, intuition, and personal experience. You will then know rather than believe.

If there is only one Reality and everything and all of the processes of life are aspects of it, why is there confusion and suffering in the world?

We can only comprehend to the extent of our capacity and most of our experiences correspond to our states of awareness and mental states and behaviors. Although the emergence of innate knowledge in the minds and awareness of individuals who comprise the global population may seem slow, it is occurring wherever it can, and will, continue to do so. In our current era, knowledge is emerging much more rapidly than in previous centuries. Conditions will improve as more people become spiritually aware.

I sometimes have the nagging thought that for me to aspire to God-realization and liberation of consciousness while there are many people in the world who need help is somewhat selfish.

The more conscious you are, the more useful your endeavors to help others will be. While attending to your own well-being and spiritual enlightenment, help others to the extent that you can. Help them in practical ways and, when possible, educate them so that they will be able to help themselves.

I welcome the idea of being in my right place in life. How can I know what it is?

Examine your private thoughts and aspirations.

How do you want to live your life?

What do you want to accomplish? Why?

Do you have the necessary knowledge and skills to do what you think is best for you to do?

If more knowledge is needed, acquire it. If you need to improve your skills, do so.

If you are aware of any mental attitudes, feelings, behaviors, or personal circumstances that might interfere with your desire to be in your right place in life, replace them with supportive conditions.

As you contemplate possibilities, write your decisions and plans. Be aware of your relationship with the Infinite and have faith that as you help yourself, the forces of nature and the impulses of grace will support and provide for you. Be receptive to and thankful for the occasions of unplanned good fortune that you encounter.

How can we know that the "transcendental" states of consciousness we may experience are not merely subjective states produced by the mind or the brain?

Authentic transcendental states illumine the mind, enable us to live more effectively, and result in Self-and God-realization.

I know of several religious teachings and have learned a variety of spiritual practices. My problem is that I don't know what to believe or what is the best way for me to meditate.

Be a knower rather than a believer. See through all opinions and theories to what is true. Use meditation procedures that enable you to experience peace of mind and superconsciousness. Meditation is not a complicated process. Review chapter 3 in this book and use the practices that are most suitable for you.

I've used affirmations for years. They help me to concentrate and to feel more confident, but I haven't yet experienced results that are satisfying. How can I use affirmations more effectively?

The key to effective use of affirmations is to experience a shift of viewpoint that enables you to realize (apprehend and experience) the truth of what is affirmed.

Affirm "I am healthy" and feel healthy.

Affirm "I am prosperous" and feel prosperous.

Affirm "I am confident" and feel confident.

Affirm "I abide in the wholeness of God" and be aware of the reality and presence of God.

When you experience the desired shift of viewpoint, maintain it.

Some people say that suffering is certain to be experienced in this world. Is it really necessary to suffer?

When our awareness is ordinary, even when circumstances are pleasant the possibility of suffering exists because they can change. Suffering can be avoided by viewing life as a drama without attachment to things or events and by removing harmful subconscious influences. If there is physical discomfort, try to alleviate it while finding the cause and removing it. If someone or an event displeases you, avoid feeling emotionally hurt. Be calm while doing what is possible to create or attract favorable events. Suffering, other than physical pain, is due to lack of understanding. The only permanent solution to the problem of suffering is spiritual enlightenment.

If all knowledge of God and of cosmic processes is within us and we really can unfold and actualize our potential to know and to freely express, why is it not easier to do this?

Because of the habit of viewing ourselves as limited beings, and complacency. In a New Testament story (*Matthew* 13:45,46), God-realization is compared to "a pearl of great price" for which a man "sold all that he had" to obtain. When we say that we want to be God-realized, is our aspiration so fervent that we are willing to devote all of our attention and resources to it? Or do we want to be Self-realized and, at the same time, also want to continue to have a "normal" self-conscious existence?

I enjoy meditating and always feel better afterwards. My problem is that of adhering to a regular schedule.

The way to maintain a regular schedule is to decide to meditate regularly and do it. If this is not done, it is easy to procrastinate or to allow attention to be distracted. Resolve to meditate every day at the same time for at least six weeks and the habit will be well-established. It will then be natural for you to maintain your schedule.

When I meditate, I do not see light, hear subtle sounds, or have feelings of joy or ecstasy. Should I be concerned about this?

There is no need for concern. Meditators who have such perceptions will have to eventually transcend them. More reliable indications of spiritual growth are peace of mind, emotional stability, improved intellectual and intuitive abilities, improved functional skills, and an increasing awareness of the wholeness of life. Concentrate on knowing your real nature and the reality of God.

I sometimes feel like withdrawing from personal responsibilities and relationships and going into seclusion for as long is necessary to be Self-realized. Would this be helpful?

It is the rare person who can do this. In seclusion, you would still have to contend with your thoughts, memories, and desires. Occasions of withdrawal from mundane circumstances—for a few days or weeks— to experience the benefits of deep rest and extended periods of contemplation, are useful. The most practical thing to do is to organize your activities and set aside a hour or two each day for study and meditation. When not doing this, attend to your duties with alert attention so that your divine qualities can be actualized in everyday circumstances. If you are unable to do this, it is unlikely that you would be able to be self-disciplined enough to derive benefit from an extended duration of seclusion, even in an ideal environment.

Is everything that we experience the result of our desires or choices, or do some events have other causes?

Many of our experiences result from our desires, choices, and actions. Some events may have other causes.

Physical conditions may result from genetic or environmental influences which, if necessary, can be changed or overcome.

Some of our mental attitudes, habits, and behaviors may have been unconsciously acquired through the years. Constructive modes of thinking and behavior can be retained. What is not constructive can be renounced.

Because we share the collective consciousness of everyone in the mundane realm, it may be possible for us to be involved with events which occur because of the mental states and actions of others.

The forces of evolution also impel events that are not of our own choosing. We can choose how to relate to them.

Impulses within the wholeness of Consciousness of which we are units are also influential.

In my community, I do not know anyone who is as interested as I am in metaphysical study and spiritual practice. I feel a need for companionship and support on the path.

While it can be enjoyable to have the support of others who share our views and aspirations, this is not always possible. When it is available, it is best to be Self-reliant rather than be dependent on the presence or words of others.

What is the quickest way to be Self- and God-realized?

Discover who is asking the question. Be aware of your thoughts and feelings. Discern the difference between you and what you observe.

Notice that you are not the thoughts that arise in your mind, the feelings that emerge and subside, a physical body, personality, or the personal sense of selfhood that you have believed yourself to be. You are a changeless being perceiving changing conditions.

The primary cause of lack of Self- and God-realization is a mistaken perception of what we really are in relationship to God. When this mistake is corrected, our awareness is immediately restored to its natural, whole state.

All useful spiritual practices remove obstacles which restrict our innate inclination to be fully awake.

Mental obstacles may include subconscious conditionings and unresolved memories which blur awareness, cause thinking to be restless and disordered, contribute to emotional unrest, cloud the intellect, and suppress intuition.

Physical obstacles may be poor health, low energy reserves, an undeveloped brain, or an unrefined nervous system.

Other obstacles are any unwholesome, unethical, harmful, or useless behaviors which cause and nurture psychological conflicts and complicate our lives.

When these obstacles no longer exist, we can think rationally, live constructively, and more easily be Self- and God-realized.

Some enlightenment traditions emphasize nonattachment. How can we live without attachments?

Wholesome relationships are not denied; what is recommended is avoidance of strong mental or emotional attachments (grasping or clinging) which prevent rational thinking and interfere with effective living and spiritual growth.

I sometimes feel so overwhelmed with problems and demands on my time and resources that I don't know what to do.

First, organize your activities. Write a list of your priorities in order of importance. Focus your attention on those which are most important. Meditate at least 30 minutes each day to reduce stress and refresh your mind and body. Obtain sufficient sleep and keep your body well-nourished. Exercise regularly to increase your vital forces. Regardless of your duties and responsibilities, adhere to a daily regimen of self-care.

Be a possibility-thinker. Write a list of problems that you have and possible solutions for them. If you cannot discover a solution:

1. Sit in the silence for a few minutes until your mind is clear and your emotions are calm. Think of the problem and "expect" the solution to emerge in your awareness. Be patient. Eventually, ideas will begin to surface in your mind. Or, later, when you are doing something else, the solution may suddenly be discerned as an intuitive insight. Perhaps a casual remark made by someone will be helpful. While reading a magazine or newspaper or listening to the radio or watching a television broadcast you may be helpfully informed or what you hear or see may elicit ideas which will be useful.
2. When you have done your utmost to solve a problem and there is nothing more you can do, remove your attention from it and put it on God. Do not worry or allow anxiety to mar your soul peace. An ideal solution to the problem will either be revealed to you or God's Cosmic Mind will solve the problem for you.

I want to be happy, healthy, prosperous, and spiritually awake, yet my pessimistic mental attitude, occasional erratic behaviors, and self-limiting subconscious conditionings often prevail.

Analyze your deeper motives and drives. Do you greet each day with enthusiasm? Do you have a strong will-to-live or do you allow apathy to dominate your mind? Discipline yourself: cultivate an optimistic mental outlook; think before you act; weaken and replace destructive subconscious influences with positive thoughts and feelings. Refuse to dramatize fear, insecurity, or weakness. Clearly define your purposes and accomplish them. Your self-confidence will increase as you become more effectively functional and the effects of self-limiting beliefs, mental attitudes, and habits acquired in the past will then be neutralized.

In regard to spiritual growth: is a vegetarian diet essential?

While a vegetarian diet is not essential, it is helpful because it is healthier. Also, since harmlessness is a useful practice, choosing a vegetarian diet is one way of demonstrating compassion. When we are intent on our spiritual path, everything we do can be viewed as spiritual practice that contributes to an alert, attentive state of mind and awareness. Choose fresh, wholesome foods, prepare them with care, serve them with love, and be thankful to the universe for the nourishment it provides.

What is the best way to present these ideas to children?

Let your thoughtful words and ideal behaviors demonstrate the principles of right knowing, thinking, and living. When children are able to comprehend the basic laws of life, explain them. When they are able to read, provide them with informative books or other teaching aids without forcing the learning process. Knowledge of life is innate to every soul and will be recognized when interest in discovering it is keen and powers of perception are developed. It is not advisable to present abstract metaphysical ideas to children; let them discover the facts of life in accord with their capacity to do so.

Children can be taught to meditate to experience relaxation and mental peace. For small children, a 5 to 10 minute session will be sufficient. Young adults can meditate a little longer. Meditation can improve a child's powers of concentration and intellectual abilities.

Some people say that for spiritual growth to occur it is necessary to first have a healthy ego. Others have said that the ego should be renounced or transcended. Which of these opinions is true?

The ego is our personality-oriented sense of self-identity which enables us to make a distinction between ourselves and other selves and the world. When we are strongly ego-centered, we also feel that we are distinct from the one field of Consciousness.

Our ego is healthy when we know that we are spiritual beings expressing through a mind and body. We can then acknowledge the usefulness of the ego in enabling us to relate to the mundane realm, can respect others, and be self-confident. A healthy ego is not a problem; egotism and the characteristic mental attitudes and personal behaviors to which it contributes is a problem.

When meditating, the ego may be temporarily transcended as superconscious states become pronounced. When the ego is purified as a result of Self- and God-realization, our awareness can freely express through it without being blurred or confined.

How can I acquire more control over my states of consciousness?

Mastery of attention is the key to mastering states of conscious-ness. Train yourself to always be alert and attentive, to be aware of yourself in relationship to others and your environment, and to accu-rately perceive what you feel, hear, or observe.

Also learn to adjust your states of consciousness at will.

• Practice going to sleep at will and waking up at a chosen time.
• Practice meditation regularly until you can adjust your point of view from ordinary awareness to a superconscious state at will.

Also practice the technique of superconscious sleep. Lie on your back with your arms by your sides and relax.

• Internalize your attention at the spiritual eye.
• Move your awareness down to your throat. Relax. Then to your shoul-ders, upper arms, elbows, lower arms, hands, lower arms, elbows, upper arms, and shoulders, pausing for a moment to relax at each place. Continue to the chest, lower abdomen, hips, thighs, knees, lower legs, ankles, and feet. Come back up in reverse order. Repeat this procedure two or three times.
• While still looking into the spiritual eye, go down through chakras to the bottom of the spine, mentally chanting Om at each chakra or just being aware there. Pause for a moment at the base chakra, then ascend through the chakras to the spiritual eye and higher brain. Pause there for a moment, then again go down through the chakras, pause at the base chakra, and come back up through the chakras to the spiritual eye and higher brain. Do this a few times. Then, be simultaneously aware at the spiritual eye, higher brain, and heart chakra. Relaxed and alert, listen to the Om vibration or any subtle inner sound and drift into a meditative state for twenty minutes or longer.

You may also practice this procedure if you wake up during the night or early in the morning when you emerge from the ordinary sleep state and your mind and emotions are still calm.

During your regular sleep schedule, it can also be useful to go to sleep in a meditative mood. After restful sleep, observe that thoughts and feelings are somewhat dormant and desires and concerns about mundane matters are either absent or weak. The transitions from the waking state to sleep and from sleep to the waking state can be used to explore superconscious states.

Also practice conscious dreaming. There is no need to be overly concerned about dreams. If you become aware when you are dreaming, observe what is occurring. You may even experiment: knowing that you are dreaming you can gently will your dream body to levitate or move through a wall. You can see through "solid" dream matter, change the sequence of dream events, or expand your awareness to include vast regions of space, or the entire cosmos.

When you awaken from a dream, compare the perceptions you had while dreaming with your perceptions when you are awake. Be aware of the dreamlike characteristics of the physical realm which is not as solid and "real" as we may ordinarily presume it to be.

Some spiritually enlightened people say that, with spiritual growth, exceptional powers of perception and extraordinary abilities may be acquired. How should these powers and abilities be used?

Use them as you use your ordinary powers and abilities: wisely. If your motives are pure, there is no reason why you should not use the powers and abilities which may naturally be acquired as you progress through the stages of spiritual growth. Use them to live effectively, to accomplish worthwhile purposes, and to assist others to their highest good. Especially use them to clarify your awareness and awaken to Self- and God-realization. As your intellectual and intuitive powers improve and your innate knowledge emerges, you will know when and how to use exceptional powers of perception and extraordinary abilities in the most useful ways.

What are some of the characteristics a truth seeker should have in order to be successful on the spiritual path?

Sincerity, unwavering aspiration to be Self- and God-realized, willingness to learn and to grow to emotional maturity, self-discipline, patience, persistence, courage, faith, compassion, devotion, self-respect, respect for one's teachers, and firm resolve to continue until spiritual enlightenment that results in liberation of consciousness is permanent because flawless.

Glossary

Glossary

absolute Perfect, complete. Pure, not mixed. Not limited.

action The process of doing.

actualize To realize in action. Abilities are actualized when they are expressed. Goals are actualized when they are accomplished.

affirm Latin *affirmāre*, to strengthen. To declare to be true.

agnosticism The theory that asserts that God cannot be known, that only sense-perceived phenomena are objects of exact knowledge.

alienation Isolation; a sense of separation.

atheism Disbelief of the existence of God.

astral The field or realm of life forces, or of such phenomena.

avatar The emergence of divine qualities and powers in human form. An enlightened soul that incarnates to impart divine influences into planetary consciousness. The "universal avatar" concept is that divine qualities are unveiled and are increasingly influential as individual and collective consciousness becomes illumined.

awareness A state of being conscious of something.

ayurveda Sanskrit *ayus*, life; *veda*, knowledge. A natural way to nurture total well-being that evolved in India centuries ago.
  Ayurvedic diagnostic procedures include examination of the patient's pulse, temperature, skin condition, eyes, behavior, and psychological characteristics.
  Procedures used to restore and maintain balance of the basic mind-body constitution may include the use of foods and herbs, attitude adjustment, behavior modification, massage and other body work, meditation practice, and detoxification of the body.

Bhagavad Gita Holy or divine song, from *bhaj*, to revere or love, and *gai*, song. An allegoric literary work in which Krishna (representing enlightened consciousness) is portrayed as an avatar teaching his disciple-friend Arjuna "the eternal way of righteousness" with emphasis on knowledge, selfless service, devotion, and meditation.

bliss The sheer joy of awareness of pure being rather than a happy mental state or an emotional feeling or mood.

capacity The ability to receive, hold, or absorb.

causal realm The field of cosmic, electrical, and magnetic forces emanated from the field of Primordial Nature.

chakra Sanskrit "wheel." Any of the seven, subtle vital centers in the spine and brain, each with unique attributes.

The *first* chakra at the base of the spine has the earth element attribute. The prana frequency taste is sweet, the color is yellow, the sound is as restless buzzing of bees. Sanskrit *muladhara*, "foundation." A characteristic of this chakra is stability.

Second chakra: At the sacrum of the spine. Water element. The taste is astringent, the color is white, the sound is like that of a flute. Sanskrit *Swadhisthana*, "abode of self-consciousness." A characteristic influence is sensualness.

Third chakra: At the lumbar region of the spine opposite the navel. Fire-element. The taste is bitter, the color is red, the sound is like that of a harp. Sanskrit *Manipura*, "the city of jewels." When awareness is identified here, one may express self-control and fervent aspiration to spiritual growth.

Fourth chakra: At the dorsal region of the spine between the shoulder blades. Air element. The taste is sour, the color is blue, the sound is like a continuous peal of a gong. Sanskrit *Anahata*, "unstruck sound." When awareness is identified here, one may have mastery of the senses and of life forces.

Fifth Chakra: At the cervical region of the spine, opposite the throat. Ether (space) element. The taste is pungent, the color is grey or misty with sparkling pinpoints of white light, the sound is like the roar of the ocean. Sanskrit *Vishudda*, "pure." When awareness is identified here, one may have exceptional powers of intellectual and intuitive discernment.

Sixth Chakra: Between the eyebrows, associated with the front lobes of the brain. Life forces flowing upward and focused here may be perceived as a dark blue orb with a golden halo centered with a silver-white light. Gold is said to be the life force frequency of Om; dark blue, the frequency of all-pervading Consciousness; the white star-like light has all of the colors of light wavelengths. Sanskrit *Ajna*, "command."

Seventh Chakra: Related, but not confined, to the higher brain. Pure consciousness, transcendence of mental and physical states and of all conditions that modify or distort awareness. Sanskrit *Sahasrara*, "thousand rayed."

channeling A modern word for mediumship: the belief that souls which have departed from this world can be contacted by telepathic or other means for the purpose of communication. Some people at the second stage of soul unfoldment (see chapter 4) try to contact souls in astral realms to prove that life continues after physical death or to acquire "higher" knowledge. Their endeavors would be more spiritually useful if they, instead, concentrated on actualizing their own divine qualities. Anyone who claims to readily communicate information from departed souls is either self-deceived or dishonest. Sincere truth seekers should not indulge in such activities.

compassion Empathetic concern for the suffering or misfortune of others together with an inclination to give aid or support.

concentration An undisturbed flow of attention.

consciousness In ordinary usage, a state of being aware. When the word is spelled with an upper case *S*, it is used to refer to God or the one reality-field.

contemplate Latin *com*, intensive; *templum*, space for observing a sign or indication. To ponder or to consider as being possible. To hopefully look at with expectation.

cosmic consciousness Awareness of the unified wholeness of life.

Cosmic Mind The "one Mind" of which particularized minds are units or parts. A person's mental states, subliminal tendencies and urges, thoughts, desires, and intentions interact with Cosmic Mind which is inclined to respond by manifesting corresponding circumstances.

decisive Characterized by determined or resolute choice.

deism The belief that God created the universe, but is apart from it, has no influence on phenomena, and provides no revelation.

delusion An erroneous idea or belief.

devotion Strong attachment or loyalty to something or someone.

diligent Careful, attentive, perseverance.

disciple Latin *discipulus*, learner or student. On a spiritual path, an adherent of a philosophical system or spiritual tradition.

effect An event, circumstance, or thing produced by a cause.

ego The soul's illusional sense of selfhood that causes and sustains a mistaken sense of self-identity. When the ego is purified, one is aware of being an individualized unit of infinite Consciousness.

egotism An exaggerated sense of self importance; arrogance.

elicit To bring forth.

emotion A subjective feeling-response to something: compassion, love (attraction), aversion, fear, revulsion, elation, or any other feeling-response that one might have.

enlightenment To provide with insight and/or spiritual wisdom.

era A duration of time. See an explanation of the theory of causes and influences of time-cycles in chapter 13 of the text.

field An area is which events can occur. Our awareness is a field. Cosmic Mind is a field. The Oversoul aspect of Consciousness and the realm of Primordial Nature are fields. *Physics*: a region of space indicated by physical properties such as gravitational or electromagnetic force.

God The single Reality. The absolute aspect is Existence-Being. The expressive aspect (Godhead or Oversoul) has attributes which pervade its emanated power (Om).

The word *god* is traced via Germanic to an Indo-European language in which an ancestor form means "the invoked one." The surviving non-Germanic relative is Sanskrit *hu* (invoke the Gods), a form of which is in the Rig-Veda (Hymn of Knowledge), the most ancient of Hindu scriptures: *puru-hutas* (much invoked), characterizes the "god" (aspect of cosmic power) Indra, depicted as the ruler of thunder and lightning. The Sanskrit word *Brahma* is used to refer to the expanding, creation-producing aspect of God. The absolute aspect is referred to as *Brahman*.

Muslims, adherents of Islam who are devoted to the ideal of submission to God, use the word *Allah* (*al-Lah*), the Great Adored. Christians use the words *God, Heavenly Father,* and *Lord*.

In early Christian translations of the Old Testament, the word *Jehovah* is an altered form of Hebrew *Yahway*. The Hebrew alphabet has characters for consonants; vowels are indicated by dots or "points" above or below consonants. The Hebrew name for God, with consonants transliterated as YHWH, was considered so sacred that it was never audibly pronounced and its proper vowel points were not written. In some texts the vowel points for another word, *Adonai* (Lord), were written with YHWH to indicate that it was to be spoken instead. The early translators made the mistake of trying to pronounce *Yahway* with the wrong vowel sounds.

Names given to God (Old English, the Highest Good) reflect what people imagined as the highest attribute of deity. Zoroastrians (in ancient Persia, now Iran) used *Ahura Mazda*, the Wise Creator. In Hinduism some aspects are characterized according to presumed or actual influences or roles: *Divine Mother*, nurturing influence; *Ishwara*, ruler; *Shiva*, transformative, regenerative influence; *Vishnu*, that which preserves; *Saraswati*, goddess of speech and learning; *Lakshmi*, goddess of prosperity and good fortune. Each "goddess" is depicted as the creative energy (shakti) of the "gods," the cosmic forces and their unique influences.

Godhead The Oversoul aspect of supreme Consciousness. The first self-manifested aspect with constituent attributes which emanates its vibrating power (Om) that produced and sustains the universe.

grace Freely given benefits, good fortune, provision, or support.

guna A constituent attribute of Consciousness in its manifest aspect which regulates cosmic forces. Three influences are described as 1) illuminating; 2) transformative; 3) inertial.

guru That which removes darkness. A teacher. In enlightenment traditions a guru is viewed as a conduit through which Self-realized knowledge and transformative spiritual force can be transmitted to receptive disciples.

hallucination A false or distorted perception of objects or events with a strong sense of their reality. Mind-produced phenomena which does not have any real basis.

heart The central part, the essence of one's being.

humility Absence of egotism.

illusion Latin *illusio,* an imitation or counterfeit of something. A mistaken perception of subjective or objective reality: of thoughts, concepts, feelings, or external things or events.

imagination A mental picture or concept of something which does not yet exist or does not exist in the present environment. Fantasy is unregulated imagination.

initiation A "new beginning." Many life-enhancing experiences or events can be considered as an initiation. In an enlightenment tradition, formal initiation is the occasion of acceptance into the company of others who are adherents of specific teachings as well as when personal instruction in spiritual practice is imparted.

inspired Latin *inspirāre: in-,* into, and *spirāre,* to breath. To be guided, affected, or aroused by divine influence.

intellect The faculty of discrimination or discernment.

intuition Direct perception without the aid of the senses.

karma An influence that can cause effects to occur. Accumulated mental conditionings and influential subliminal tendencies and urges comprise one's personal karmic condition (which is of the mind, not of the true Self).

kundalini Soul force. In people who are not yet spiritually awake, it is mostly dormant. In spiritually awake people, its energies are active, transformative, and empowering. Its energies are aroused by aspiration to spiritual growth, devotion, meditation and other practices, being in places where spiritual forces are strong, and mental and spiritual attunement with an enlightened person.

life The physical, mental, and spiritual experiences that make up our sense of existence.

light Electromagnetic radiation. Light travels at 186,000 miles per second. The sun's electromagnetic radiation travels 93 million miles in almost 8 minutes to our planet where we perceive some of it as visible light when it impacts earth's magnetic field.

mantra From Sanskrit *manas*, mind; and *tra*, to protect. A word, word-phrase, or sound used to focus attention when meditating.

material A substance of which something is made.

matter Something that occupies space. Matter is energy confined in a small space.

meditation An undisturbed flow of attention to an object or ideal to be identified with or realized. Intentional detachment of attention and awareness from external conditions, the senses, emotions, and mental states that enables one to realize the pure-conscious essence of being and the reality of God.

metaphysics Latin *metaphysica* < Greek *Ta meta ta phusika*, the things after the physics, the title of Aristotle's treatise on first principles, so-called because it followed his work on physics. The branch of philosophy that investigates the nature of first principles of ultimate reality, including study of the nature of being and cosmology.

mind The faculty used to process perceptions and information.

modify To change the character of something. To limit or restrict. Our ordinary awareness is modified by acquired information, erroneous opinions, misperceptions of facts, sleep, and memories. Pure awareness of being, transcendent superconsciousness, is unmodified.

mysticism Spiritual discipline practiced to experience unification of awareness with God or ultimate reality by contemplative meditation. The experience of such realization. Belief in the existence of realities beyond ordinary powers of perception which are accessible by subjective experience, as by intuition.

Om The vibration of the power of Consciousness. In some religious traditions Om is referred to as God's Word.

omnipotence Unlimited power.

omnipresence Present everywhere.

omniscience All knowing.

Oversoul See *Godhead*.

prana Life force that sustains and animates living things.

pranayama Sanskrit *pran*, life force; *ayama*, not restrained. The formal practice of pranayama usually involves regulation of breathing rhythms to harmonize flows of life force in the body and calm the mind as preparation for meditation practice.

Primordial Nature The first field of cosmic manifestation in which Om and its self-manifested aspects—space, time, and cosmic forces—are unified.

prosperity Having success, thriving. When the spiritual, mental, emotional, physical, and environmental components of our lives are harmoniously integrated, we are truly prosperous.

psyche In Western cultures the *psyche* (Latin from Greek *psūkhe*, soul) is usually viewed as "the mind functioning as the center of thought, feeling, and behavior and consciously or unconsciously adjusting and relating the body to its social and physical environment." A soul (the original meaning of the word) in one part of the world is not different from a soul in another part of the world. How people are conditioned to view themselves in relationship to God and the world and how they think and act often differs.

The practical means by which obstacles to spiritual growth can be removed are the same and can be used by everyone. When first learning about spiritual practices that evolved in other regions of the world, some people have difficulty grasping new philosophical concepts or the words used to describe them. Or they may falsely presume that cultural behaviors unlike their own must be adopted. Acquired mental attitudes and habits may also be a problem: in cultures where self-reliance and a strong sense of individualism is emphasized, resistance to having a teacher or to purifying the ego may be obstacles to learning and spiritual growth.

realization Accurate comprehension by direct perception and personal experience.

redemptive The capacity to restore, rescue, free or liberate.

reincarnation The return of souls to physical embodiment because of necessity or the soul's inclination to have experiences here. It is not spiritually beneficial to be overly concerned about possible, previous, or future earth-sojourns. Our attention and endeavors should instead be focused on authentic spiritual growth that will result in liberation of consciousness.

salvation A condition of liberation from pain or discomfort, which may be temporary or permanent in accord with one's degree of Self- and God-realization.

samadhi Oneness, wholeness. Preliminary meditative samadhi is usually supported by an object of perception. Transcendent states are devoid of perceived, supporting objects.

science Orderly, disciplined observation, identification, description, and experimental investigation of mundane phenomena or of higher realities.

seer One who clearly discerns the truth of what is observed.

Self An individualized unit of pure consciousness; the core essence of being. Our true nature, rather the illusional sense of selfhood (ordinary self-consciousness). When identified with matter and a mind and body the Self is referred to as a soul. Units of pure consciousness are individualized when interactions between the spirit or life of God and Primordial Nature enable the inertial attribute of Consciousness to be influential. Self-realization occurs when one can discern the difference between the essence of being and ordinary awareness.

soul See *Self.*

space The infinite extension of three-dimensional reality in which events occur.

spiritual Of or related to God and souls.

stage A level, degree, or period of time in the course of a process.

subjective Existing only in one's mind or awareness.

subliminal Below the threshold of conscious awareness. Subliminal drives and tendencies activate thoughts and emotions. When they are pacified, the mind is calm and awareness is clear.

superconscious Latin *super*, above or over. Superconscious states are superior to ordinary states of consciousness.

technique A systematic procedure. A meditation technique can be used to elicit relaxation, calm the mind, and focus attention.

time An interval between events. A part of a continuum (wholeness) which includes space and cosmic forces, no part of which can be distinguished from the others except by arbitrary (individual judgment) division for the purpose of analysis or for theoretical speculation.

    Our concept of time is related to things and events: pendulums swing; quartz crystals vibrate; atoms, light waves, electric and magnetic fields and planets move. But what is time like in a void where nothing exists? In an absolute void only the Something that makes relative happenings possible exists.

    The interval of time we call a year marks one revolution of the earth around the sun; a day is one spin of the earth around its axis;

a month was once related to the duration of the orbit of the moon. Astronomical measures of time are not absolute because they are constantly changing. The moon is farther away from the earth than it was many thousands of years ago. Five hundred million years ago, a day was about twenty hours long. Days and years are variable happenings rather than exact markings of time. Our seven-day week is arbitrary. Through the ages, various cultures have had five day, eight day, and ten day weeks.

Until the fourteenth century, days were divided into irregular intervals of morning, noon, evening, and night. Summer daylight hours were (and are) longer than winter daylight hours. Hours and minutes and time zones began to be standardized only a few centuries ago, so that train and other schedules could be determined.

At the Equator, the earth's rate of spin on its axis is 1000 miles an hour and its speed around the sun is almost 20 miles a second (72,000 miles an hour). Our solar system in relationship to the center of our galaxy is moving at the rate of 120 miles a second (432,000 miles an hour). Our galaxy is moving toward another galaxy (Andromeda) at 50 miles a second (180,000 miles an hour).

Time need not be thought of as an insurmountable obstacle to spiritual growth which can be slow, faster, or rapid in accord with the capacity of the individual and one's intensity of endeavor. Refinements of the nervous system, however, and other physical changes that may be necessary to accommodate higher states of consciousness, occur in time.

transcendental Rising above common thought, ideas, or stages of consciousness. Interest in the underlying basis of knowledge.

Transcendental Field Absolute or pure Consciousness. Defined as Existence-Being because it does not have attributes. The ultimate stage of God-realization.

transcendentalism The belief that knowledge of reality is derived from intuitive sources rather than wholly by objective experience.

worthwhile Valuable or important enough to justify expenditure of effort or resources.

wisdom Understanding of what is true, right, or enduring.

yoga To "yoke" together or "unify." 1. Awareness of being unified with one field of Consciousness. 2. Samadhi, the meaning used in Patanjali's *yoga-sutras*. 3. The systems used to accomplish Self- and God-realization. Although most of its practices are based on philosophical concepts, yoga is not a religion. The practices are believed to have been originated at least five thousand years ago, in India.

Hatha Yoga practices include asanas (postures) that strengthen muscles, improve flexibility and blood and lymph circulation, mudras (procedures used to acquire a degree of conscious control over involuntary physical functions and awaken kundalini energies), pranayama, and meditation.

Bhakti Yoga is the way of love, compassion, devotion to God, and reverence for life.

Karma Yoga is the way of constructive, selfless action.

Jnana (gyana) Yoga is the way of knowledge and wisdom.

Raja (superior) Yoga is the way of contemplative meditation.

In other yogic systems, such as Kriya Yoga, special practices that include the most useful procedures of all of the systems are emphasized. *Kriya* means "action." *Kriyas* are actions performed to remove all mental and physical obstacles to Self- and God-realization (*yoga-sutras* 2:1,2).

yoga-sutras Sanskrit *sutra*, from verb-root *siv*, to sew. Sutras are "threads" of concepts that together describe a theory or explain a philosophical view.

Patanjali, who wrote the text during the second century of the current era, compiled what was then known about yogic practices and presented the information in concise, systematic form. In the first chapter, superconscious states and the means by which they can be realized are described. In the other three chapters, specific spiritual practices, their results, and stages of awakening up to and including liberation of consciousness are explained.

ROY EUGENE DAVIS, the founder-director of Center for Spiritual Awareness, is widely known for his clear, mature presentation of these effective spiritual growth processes.
Ordained by Paramahansa Yogananda (Los Angeles, 1951), Mr. Davis has lectured in more than 100 North American cities, Japan, West Africa, Brazil, Europe, and India. Some of his books have been published in ten languages and in eleven countries.

The international headquarters of Center for Spiritual Awareness is located in the northeast Georgia mountains, ninety miles from Atlanta. Facilities include the offices and publishing department, a meeting hall and dining room, the Shrine of All Faiths Meditation Temple, libraries, and six comfortable guest houses. Meditation retreats are offered from early spring until late autumn.

For a free information packet and book list, contact:

Center for Spiritual Awareness
Post Office Box 7
Lakemont, Georgia 30552-0001

Telephone 706-782-4723 weekdays 8 a.m. to 4 p.m.
Fax 706-782-4560
E-mail: csainc@csa-davis.org
Internet Web Site: www.csa-davis.org

Recommended Supplemental Reading
Books by Roy Eugene Davis

SEVEN LESSONS IN CONSCIOUS LIVING
A Progressive Program of Higher Learning and Spiritual Practice in the Kriya Yoga Tradition
  Philosophy, lifestyle guidelines, and meditation techniques and routines for all levels of practice. 8-1/2 x 11 workbook format.
                                    Softbound, 144 pages, $10.00
THE PATH OF LIGHT
A Guide to 21st Century Discipleship and Spiritual Practice in the Kriya Yoga Tradition
  The philosophical principles, lifestyle guidelines, meditation practices, and initiation procedures of this timeless enlightenment path. And a new presentation of Patanjali's yoga-sutras.
                                    Hardcover, 160 pages, $7.95
THE ETERNAL WAY
The Inner Meaning of the Bhagavad Gita
  The Bhagavad Gita is an important scripture of yoga. In eighteen illuminating chapters, the means by which authentic spiritual growth may be accomplished are clearly described for aspirants at every level of psychological and spiritual growth.   Hardcover, 320 pages, $14.95

AN EASY GUIDE TO AYURVEDA
The Natural Way to Wholeness
  Understanding and Balancing the Mind-Body Constitution - Food Choices - Cleansing Routines - Rejuvenation, Enlightened Living, and Immortality. Colors, gemstones, metals, and mantras: their special qualities and applications according to ancient traditions and modern discoveries.   Softbound, 160 pages, $4.95

Postage and handling, $2.00 for one book; 30 cents for each extra book.
Outside the U.S., double these amounts for airmail.

CSA Press P.O. Box 7 Lakemont, Georgia 30552-0001

Telephone 706-782-4723 Weekdays 8 a.m. to 4 p.m.
Fax 706-782-4560 anytime   E-mail: csainc@csa-davis.org
Internet Web Site: www.csa-davis.org

Request a Free Book Catalog